The Peaceful Stillness
OF THE
Silent Mind

Previously published by the LAMA YESHE WISDOM ARCHIVE

Becoming Your Own Therapist, by Lama Yeshe
Advice for Monks and Nuns, by Lama Yeshe and Lama Zopa Rinpoche
Virtue and Reality, by Lama Zopa Rinpoche
Make Your Mind an Ocean, by Lama Yeshe
Teachings from the Vajrasattva Retreat, by Lama Zopa Rinpoche
Daily Purification: A Short Vajrasattva Practice, by Lama Zopa Rinpoche
The Essence of Tibetan Buddhism, by Lama Yeshe
Making Life Meaningful, by Lama Zopa Rinpoche
Teachings from the Mani Retreat, by Lama Zopa Rinpoche
Direct and Unmistaken Method, by Lama Zopa Rinpoche
The Yoga of Offering Food, by Lama Zopa Rinpoche

For initiates only:

A Chat about Heruka, by Lama Zopa Rinpoche
A Chat about Yamantaka, by Lama Zopa Rinpoche

In association with TDL Publications, Los Angeles:

Mirror of Wisdom, by Geshe Tsultim Gyeltsen
Illuminating the Path to Enlightenment, by His Holiness the Dalai Lama

May whoever sees, touches, reads, remembers, or talks or thinks about these books never be reborn in unfortunate circumstances, receive only rebirths in situations conducive to the perfect practice of Dharma, meet only perfectly qualified spiritual guides, quickly develop bodhicitta and immediately attain enlightenment for the sake of all sentient beings.

LAMA YESHE

THE PEACEFUL STILLNESS OF THE SILENT MIND

Buddhism, Mind and Meditation

Edited by Nicholas Ribush

LAMA YESHE WISDOM ARCHIVE • BOSTON

www.LamaYeshe.com

A non-profit charitable organization for the benefit of all sentient beings and a section of the Foundation for the Preservation of the Mahayana Tradition

www.fpmt.org

First published 2004
15,000 copies for free distribution

LAMA YESHE WISDOM ARCHIVE
PO BOX 356
WESTON
MA 02493 USA

ISBN 1-891868-14-4

10 9 8 7 6 5 4 3 2 1

Front cover photo Carol Royce-Wilder
Back cover photo Ueli Minder
Line drawings Chapter 3 Peter Griffin
Designed by Mark Gatter

Please contact the LAMA YESHE WISDOM ARCHIVE for more free
copies of this book

CONTENTS

1. BUDDHISM: SOMETHING FOR EVERYBODY   13

2. SPIRITUALITY AND MATERIALISM   27

3. EXPERIENCING SILENT WISDOM   41

4. ATTITUDE IS MORE IMPORTANT THAN ACTION   57

5. AN INTRODUCTION TO MEDITATION   73

6. FOLLOW YOUR PATH WITHOUT ATTACHMENT   87

GLOSSARY   109

Benefactor's Dedication

Generous Americans contribute substantially to organizations whose missions are to rid the world of horrid diseases. For my wife Eleanor and me, our cause of choice was a mystifying disease called myasthenia gravis, or, as we call it, MG.

We became involved with the MG Foundation of California because we were impressed with the indomitable spirit of the patients who waged daily battle against this illness and the incredibly dedicated volunteers seeking to cure it. Myasthenia is Latin for muscle weakness and gravis Greek for grave. Symptoms include drooping eyelids, double vision, slurred speech and, in more severe cases, breathing difficulties.

Eleanor once observed the empathy among patients at an MG education meeting and commented, "Knowing that others share the experience of this illness is clearly a unifying force for them." Their determination to retain self-esteem and dignity despite the ravages of their disease is why we were devoted volunteers and generous donors to the MG cause for 20 years.

Sadly, my beautiful Eleanor passed from this life in April of 2003 and so I dedicate this book to her for the 43 years of unconditional love she gave me. Eleanor was blessed with nearly 90 years on this Earth, mostly in good health. She felt strongly that people should be "giving while living." Perhaps her longevity could be attributed to her generosity and caring spirit. With Eleanor's passing, the MG Foundation lost an outstanding supporter and I lost a most significant part of me.

—John W. Allen

PUBLISHER'S ACKNOWLEDGMENTS

We are extremely grateful to our friends and supporters who have made it possible for the LAMA YESHE WISDOM ARCHIVE to both exist and function: to Lama Yeshe and Lama Zopa Rinpoche, whose kindness is impossible to repay; to Peter and Nicole Kedge and Venerable Ailsa Cameron for helping bring the ARCHIVE to its present state of development; to Venerable Roger Kunsang, Lama Zopa's tireless assistant, for his kindness and consideration; and to our sustaining supporters: Drs. Penny Noyce & Leo Liu, Barry & Connie Hershey, Joan Terry, Roger & Claire Ash-Wheeler, Claire Atkins, Doren & Mary Harper, Tom & Suzanne Castles, Hawk Furman, Richard Gere, Lily Chang Wu and Thubten Yeshe.

In particular, we would like to thank John W. Allen for compassionately sponsoring this title in memory of his late wife, Eleanor Allen.

We are also deeply grateful to those who have also been major contributors or book sponsors over the past few years: Dean Alper, Christine Arlington, Peggy Bennington, Dharmawati Brechbuhl, Ross Brooke, Rose Canfield, the Caytons (Lori, Karuna, Pam, Bob & Amy), Lai-Hing Chong, Ngawang Chotak, Kok Leng Chuah, John Clulow, Denise Dagley, Paula de Wijs-Koolkin, Chris Dornan, Cecily Drucker, Derek & Soon Hui Goh, Dan & Tara Bennett Goleman, Lorraine Greenfield, Richard F. Hay, Heruka Center, Su Hung, Ecie Hursthouse, Barbara Jenson, Kadampa Center, Bill Kelly & Robyn Brentano, Eric Klaft, Tony LaGreca, Land of Medicine Buddha, Chiu-Nan Lai, Chiu-Mei Lai, Henry & Catherine Lau, Salim Lee, Harry Leong (in loving memory of his father, Woon Leong), Mony & Ester Liberman, SS Lim, Judy Mindrol Lin, Jamieson Lowe, Sandra Magnussen, Doss McDavid, Kathleen McDonald, Ellen McInerney, Amy McKhann, Petra McWilliams, Tara Melwani, Therese Miller, Lynda Millspaugh, Ueli Minder, Janet Moore, Jack Morison, Esther Ngai, Trong Nguyen, Gerard O'Halloran, Dennis Paulson, James Pelkey, Leslie Reincke, Dorian Ribush, Claire Ritter, Ven. Ingeborg Sandberg, Mayra Rocha Sandoval, Jesse Sartain, Jack Sonnabaum & Judith Hunt,

Datuk Tai Tsu Kuang, Tan Swee Eng, Tom Thorning, Thubten Norbu Ling Center, Tushita Retreat Centre, Wendy van den Heuvel, Diana van Die (in loving memory of Lenie van Die), Oanh Vovan, Tom Waggoner & Renee Robison, Vajrapani Institute, Robbie Watkins and Wisdom Publications.

We would like, as well, to express our appreciation for the kindness and compassion of all those other generous benefactors mentioned in detail in our previous publications and those who have contributed funds to our work since our last published list a couple of years ago. They are too numerous to mention individually in this book, but we value highly each and every donation made to spreading the Dharma for the sake of the kind mother sentient beings and now pay tribute to you all on our Web site, www.LamaYeshe.com. Thank you so much.

I would also like to pay tribute here to our dear and long-time friend and supporter who helped us and many other Dharma and Tibet-related projects for almost thirty years, Carol Davies, who passed way in Perth earlier this year, far too soon. May she and all other sentient beings immediately realize bodhicitta and quickly attain supreme enlightenment.

I would also like to thank the many kind people who have asked that their donations be kept anonymous; the volunteers who have given so generously of their time to help us with our mailings, especially Therese Miller; my wife, Wendy Cook, for her tireless help and support; our dedicated office staff, Jennifer Barlow and Linda Merle; Alison Ribush & Mandala Books (Melbourne) and Veronica Kaczmarowski & FPMT Australia for much appreciated assistance with our work in Australia; and Dennis Heslop, Philip Bradley and our other friends at Wisdom Books (London) for their great help with our work in Europe. We appreciate, too, the kindness and expertise of our main volunteer transcribers, Su Hung, Segen Speer-Senner and Gareth Robinson. We also thank most sincerely Massimo Corona and the FPMT International Office for their generous financial and administrative assistance.

Finally, I want to express my gratitude to Greg Sneddon and his wonderful team of volunteers in Melbourne, Australia—

including Dr. Su Hung, Anne Pottage, Llysse Valez, Chris Friedl and Anthony Deague—who recently completed digitizing almost our entire archive of more than 10,000 hours of teachings by Lama Yeshe and Lama Zopa Rinpoche and will continue to help us in this area.

Special gratitude is extended to the wonderful Mark Gatter for his invaluable help and fine esthetic in the design and production of this and most of our other books.

If you, dear reader, would like to join this noble group of open-hearted altruists by contributing to the production of more free books by Lama Yeshe or Lama Zopa Rinpoche or to any other aspect of the LAMA YESHE WISDOM ARCHIVE's work, please contact us to find out how.

—*Dr. Nicholas Ribush*

Through the merit of having contributed to the spread of the Buddha's teachings for the sake of all sentient beings, may our benefactors and their families and friends have long and healthy lives, all happiness, and may all their Dharma wishes be instantly fulfilled.

Lama Yeshe and the editor on the road to Lawudo, Nepal, May 1973

EDITOR'S INTRODUCTION

Welcome to the Lama Yeshe Wisdom Archive's fourth free book of teachings by Lama Yeshe. I'm sure we'll have as much trouble keeping this title in print as we've had with our previous publications, *Becoming Your Own Therapist*, *Make Your Mind an Ocean* and *The Essence of Tibetan Buddhism*, all of which we've recently reprinted, the first two in a now combined edition. *The Peaceful Stillness of the Silent Mind* brings to more than 150,000 Lama Yeshe books we have published for free distribution, something we can all rejoice in. Sincere and grateful thanks to all those who have made this possible.

The six teachings contained herein come from Lama Yeshe's 1975 visit to Australia. The first three are a series of consecutive evening lectures Lama gave at Melbourne University. By the third night he thought people had heard enough talk and instead offered a guided meditation. We have indicated the breaks clearly and suggest that instead of reading it straight through, you pause for a few minutes after each paragraph to think about what Lama just said, as he intended.

The last three teachings are public lectures given in Sydney. Again, they are filled with love, insight, wisdom and compassion, and the question-answer sessions Lama loved so much are as dynamic and informative as ever. We hope you'll enjoy reading these talks as much as we delight in bringing them to you.

Once more, I thank Wendy Cook and Linda Gatter for their kind and helpful editorial suggestions.

Vajrapani Institute, July 1983

1

BUDDHISM: SOMETHING FOR EVERYBODY

Some people think they know all about Buddhism and Buddhists just because they've read a couple of books. They pick one up, "Hmm. Let's see what this book says. Well, according to this it seems that Buddhists are really extreme. They believe in all sorts of strange stuff." They pick up another: "My goodness, Buddhists are completely nihilistic." They draw all sorts of wrong conclusions based on extremely limited information; they don't see anything like the whole picture. This is very dangerous.

Perhaps they read something from the Madhyamaka school of Buddhist philosophy, which is known for its rigorous intellectual approach to the subject of emptiness, the ultimate nature of reality, and can be very difficult to understand. This can lead them to think, "Oh, Buddhists aren't religious; they're atheists. They don't believe anything; they think that nothing exists. How can they consider themselves religious?" This too can be very dangerous.

Other people might conclude, "Wow! Buddhists believe in three Gods. They say Buddha is one God; Dharma is another; Sangha a third. They must be super-believers. That's too much. In the West, we've never heard of such a thing as three Gods; only one. We're religious, but we only have one God. We can't even agree with the Buddhists on how many Gods there are."

If you look at just one tiny aspect of Buddhism, of course it might appear too much for you. But Buddhism is not just about one or two small things; it is not some tiny philosophy. Lord Buddha explained the nature of every single phenomenon in the universe.

At this stage, I have had about nine or ten years' experience teaching Buddhist philosophy to Westerners and experimenting with how it fits their minds, mainly in the one-month meditation courses we hold each year at Kopan Monastery in Nepal. In these courses we try to explain everything, but I have found that if we talk too much about the negative side of things, students completely freak out. Not all of them, but many do. They say, "These lamas emphasize the negative too much. Why don't they talk more about the positive? Buddhism isn't only about delusion and suffering. Why do they teach us this negative stuff day after day?"

But the thing about Buddhism is that before you can put yourself into the positive path to liberation, enlightenment or God—whatever you want to call it, the name doesn't matter—you have to know how your negative mind works.

If you don't understand how the two extreme negative views of overestimation and underestimation function within you, how can you correct your actions and put yourself into the right path? Therefore, it is crucial to know the negative aspects of your nature. Actually, if you comprehend the evolution of your negative mind from beginning to end, you'll feel very comfortable. Conversely, if you don't know how it works, you'll finish up thinking that negative actions are positive.

Moreover, if you try to practice the path to liberation without a solid grounding in what is positive and what is negative, a simple question from someone challenging what you are doing can completely derail you. You might get confused and give up. That's the sign of a weak mind. You have to see the totality of the evolution of both the negative and the positive mind.

Some people assume that Buddhism is probably a nice religion that always talks diplomatically and sweetly about holy things. When we start teaching Buddhism to beginners, we don't begin by talking about holy things. The first thing we explain is the basic nature of your present mind—what's going on down here, right now—not Buddha up there.

However, at this point, I would like to say one thing about the nature of Buddha. As I mentioned before, some people with a limited knowledge of Buddhism think that while Christianity and other religions say that God is only one, Buddhists worship three Gods. Actually, if you understand the true nature of Buddha, Dharma and Sangha, you'll know that there's no separation between them. Buddha is Buddha; Buddha is Dharma; Buddha is Sangha. Accepting Buddha, Dharma and Sangha as the ultimate refuge does not contradict the unity of God.

There are those who think that Buddhism is simply an intellectual philosophy and includes no religious practice. That's not true either. Buddhism contains both intellectual philosophy and religious practice. When Lord Buddha was teaching, he taught his students as individuals, giving each whatever they needed. When offering solutions to the negative mind, he would reveal different methods, because each person's negative mind is different. Sometimes he would explain, "Yes, this exists," but at others he would say, "No, this doesn't exist," drawing upon the Buddhist school of thought appropriate for each person's level of mind.

Seeing this, people whose minds are limited might think that Lord Buddha was confused, that his explanations were contradictory. But Lord Buddha was not confused. He was a wise teacher who could see that different minds experienced different problems and, therefore, different solutions were required. For example, a skillful doctor might advise a patient with a fever to fast for a couple of days but then tell the patient to eat. The small-minded person might observe, "This doctor is silly. One day he says don't eat, the next day he says eat. He's really confused." But actually, the doctor is wise. He understands the evolution of the patient's disease, so he prescribes different treatments at different times.

Lord Buddha, the supreme physician, treated his disciples the same way. He taught sentient beings according to their level of mind. You can't all of a sudden start talking about the intellectual intricacies of the enlightened view to people whose minds are completely confused. They have a long way to go; they have to be taught what their limited minds can digest. If even Lord Buddha were to teach you things your mind could not digest, you'd freak out. Instead of gaining benefit, you'd go berserk. You have to know this.

Even before Buddhism came to Tibet, there were already many different Buddhist schools, doctrines and philosophies in existence. There still are. But basically, they are in no way contradictory. They are all there for the gradual development of the human mind. Actually, all those various doctrines and philosophies exist for the gradual development of the individual person's mind.

In the lowest school of Buddhist philosophy, Lord Buddha teaches that phenomena are self-existent. In the next, he teaches that they are not completely self-existent; that something comes from the side of the object and something from the side of the mind. Finally, he explains that in reality, nothing at all comes from the side of the object; it exists only in name.

You'll find that some religions don't have these different levels of view; don't have a variety of approaches for the gradual development of the human mind. In Buddhism, when your mind is at the initial level you are given certain practices to do. When, through those practices, your mind has developed a little, you are taught the methods of the next level. When you have accomplished those, you go on to more advanced techniques. In this way, by degrees, your understanding and perception change and you progress along the path. Thus, Buddhism is extremely precise. Whoever you are, you can find specific philosophical explanations and methods of practice to suit your individual level of mind.

In the West, we pick up a book, "Oh, this sounds good. I like this book. I think I'll practice this meditation." But even though the words sound nice and you like the ideas, if you're not ready for a certain practice, there's no way you can integrate it with your mind, and if you try, you might end up thinking, "Oh, this method doesn't work." But the problem is not with the method; it's with your trying to implement something for which you are not ready. You don't know how to integrate that idea with your mind or put it into your experience. That's the problem.

You can find nice ideas in every book in the world, but how do these nice ideas relate to your mind? How do you put them into everyday experience? If you can, it makes sense for you to practice them. Your mind will become soft and gentle, calm and peaceful, and your life will be happier. You will begin to taste the honey of Dharma. Otherwise, no honey, just Coca-Cola. Too much Coke, too much gas. No sleep and all running to the bathroom. I'm joking! I'm not talking about the physical here; these are just examples for the mind.

Whatever you find in Buddhist philosophy and practice is there solely for the psychological treatment of the human mind. Lord Buddha never propounded any abstruse philosophy just so that he could proudly proclaim, "This is my doctrine." He never propounded a single philosophical point that wasn't related to the human mind or meant to be integrated with it. Never. Buddhism is a way of living your life that is related to your own mind, your own view, your own experience. Therefore, be careful when you evaluate Buddhism as "this, this or that."

For example, after this lecture, you're going to go home and tell people, "Buddhism is this, Buddhism is that, because this Tibetan lama said so." But please don't think that tonight I've told you all about Buddhism. I've barely scratched the surface. What I'm saying here is by no means the measure of Buddhism.

Since the different schools of Buddhist philosophy and their views are graduated—different schools for different minds—how do you know that when you pick up a particular book, what it contains will fit your mind? Of course, in Lord Buddha's teachings there are methods for each of us. If you are wise, you can certainly select a book that suits you. In Buddhism, there's something for everybody—something anybody can understand and actualize—and nothing that is too difficult for anybody, that no human mind can understand. Lord Buddha gave precise teachings that can be understood by any individual according to their level of mind—different methods, different views, different philosophies, different doctrines.

For example, Lord Buddha gave a general explanation of how karma functions in everyday life that you don't need a sophisticated intellect to understand. In his very first teaching, on the four noble truths, he explained karma very simply. First, he explained true suffering. Isn't that sensible? If someone describes your own agitated mind—how it comes, how it goes, what sort of effects it has—how can you reject that? "Oh, that's too much for me." Impossible. How can you reject somebody's telling you correctly and in detail how your mind is agitated; how it's in conflict every day of your life because it is split, not integrated? If someone gives you a perfect explanation of this, how can you say it's too difficult to understand?

We don't try to teach beginners the intricacies of Madhyamaka philosophy. We can tell immediately who's ready to listen to teachings on emptiness and who isn't. But we can teach them about the problems they face every day of their lives and the nature of true suffering in such a way that they can understand the evolution of their everyday reality.

Actually, Lord Buddha taught about human suffering and the agitated mind in many different ways. To some people, he gave very simple explanations; to others, who were more intellectually advanced, he gave more subtle, technical explanations. Even the way he taught about the nature of suffering is fantastic—he had so many different approaches to introduce this subject to the human mind. Isn't it amazing? How can you deny your agitated mind? "I don't believe I have an agitated mind. I don't want to hear about that." How can you deny it? Every day of your life you are trapped in your physical body and have to put up with it. When somebody explains its nature to you, how can you reject it?

Perhaps you're going to argue that you don't have an agitated mind. In that case, I'm going to say, check how you are when you get up in the morning. Be aware for just a day, then you'll see. Or not even a day. Just try sitting still for an hour in a cross-legged position. Your ego will completely freak out: "Oh, my knees hurt." Pain in the knees is so transient; your agitated mind keeps going and going and going—all day and all night; for months, for years. It never stops.

In Sanskrit, the word for Lord Buddha's teaching is Dharma. Dharma is medicine. Just as every physical illness has its own medicine, Lord Buddha has prescribed a specific method for each mental disease. That's what he taught. He didn't just hand out the same teaching to everybody, irrespective of who they were or what their problem was. Therefore, you can't simply say, "Buddhism is this." Dharma is not just one thing.

As I mentioned before, there are various schools of Buddhist thought. The two main ones are the Hinayana and the Mahayana. The Mahayana, in turn, is divided into Paramitayana and Vajrayana, or Tantrayana. Tantrayana, or tantra, also contains a variety of schools. Basically, there are four, each of which contains its own specific techniques, but I can't go into that here. Nevertheless, it's important for you to know that there exists such a well-organized, step-by-step path, by which you can gradually develop your mind to enlightenment. Since Tibetan Buddhism is not yet perfectly established in this part of the world, I'm just mentioning this for your information.

For example, these days we have advanced modes of transport, like fast cars and jet planes, but that doesn't mean there's no longer any place for the bicycle. In the evolution of human transport, we started off with simple carts, then came cars, then planes and now we have moon rockets and so forth. Soon there'll be something to top even the rockets of today; don't think that they're the ultimate human invention. There's no limit to how far the human mind can develop. Like today, everybody has television, but a few decades ago, if you'd described a television set to somebody, they would not have believed such a thing possible. Or nowadays, in developed countries at least, many people have a car. Perhaps in time, all these people will have their own jet. You're going to tell me that that's not possible, but why not? These things are material phenomena and if the human mind puts effort in that direction, such things can develop. It's nothing supernatural; it just hasn't happened yet.

Anyway, what I'm saying is that just as here, with these material things, there are degrees of development and the earlier versions don't conflict with the later ones, so too the philosophies, doctrines, views and methods contained in Lord Buddha's profound teaching are all there for the gradual spiritual development of any one individual and do not conflict with or contradict each other.

Of course, if you think that the material sense world that you perceive is all that exists and that there's no possibility of accomplishing that which you can imagine, that it's all purely mental speculation, that's ridiculous. Even the inventor of the rocket had to picture it in his mind before he could create it. First he dreamed it up; then he put together the material elements necessary to manufacture it; then the rocket appeared. There's no way he could have made a rocket without first creating it in his mind. So you can see, all these different modern inventions result from the power of the human mind. Therefore, don't think that dreams never become reality. It's possible.

Perhaps that's enough for now. Basically, Mahayana Buddhism contains many methods and techniques and every single one is necessary for the development of each human mind. I'm not going to go into the specifics here, but if you have any questions I'd be glad to try to answer them.

Q. I'd like to ask something about reincarnation. Some occultists believe that if you're born in a Western country, you're born there for the lessons that are to be learned in the West and to take up an Eastern teaching is to regress, because you would already have been in the East many times before. Now, this might be a silly view, but some people hold it and I wonder what you think.

Lama. Well, that's a good question—I guess! So, what's your conclusion? That those born in the West are advanced human beings and for them to learn Eastern philosophy is to descend into the animal realm? That's what it sounds like. But it's a good question; some people might think like that. And I agree that there could be somebody who says, "I'm fed up with the Western way of life. I can't stand it any longer. I'm going East." This person is too extreme, and his rejecting the West and adopting Eastern ideas in this way could be seen as a return to the animal realm.

But another Westerner might think, "I have everything. I'm well educated, I have a wife and family, a good job, a house, a car and plenty of money, but I'm still not satisfied. When I was a kid, I thought if I had all this I'd be happy, but I'm not. Money is not everything. I need to support my mind." He knows the entire Western experience from beginning to end but he's still not satisfied and wants to learn about the mind. So, where can he go? He knows that Western psychologists cannot explain the nature of the mind and how it works in the present moment. But he needs satisfaction right now. He wants to be able to face the world and support his mind without fear. He checks around and comes to the conclusion that Eastern ways of thought can help him more than those of the West. Coming to Eastern philosophy in this way is progress, not a regression to the animal realm. For some people, it's necessary. Therefore, taking up Eastern thought can be positive for some, while for others it can be negative.

Q. Scientists say that there are intelligent beings throughout the universe. Is Earth the only place where people can gain enlightenment or do you consider that there are intelligent beings on other planets who can gain enlightenment in their own physical plane?
Lama. It's not only in this solar system that you can get enlightened. Both science and Lord Buddha have described billions and billions of solar systems. What Lord Buddha described 2,500 years ago and what the scientists of today have discovered have come together perfectly.

Q. Have you ever been reincarnated? Have you had previous lives?
Lama. Yes, of course. My mind—but not this body—has come from previous lives. And I'll go on forever. This life will become a past life of my future ones. Nothing can stop the energy of consciousness, or mind. Therefore, killing yourself is no solution to a difficult life. It's much better to simply relax and wait for death to come in its own time.

Q. Does Buddhism teach an end to a particular mind or does the transfer of minds go on forever?
Lama. Some kinds of mind can end but there's no end to the basic mind. The moment-to-moment mind—the waves upon the ocean—can stop but the energy of the ocean of mind runs forever.

Q. Does that mean that the world and the universe will continue infinitely?

Lama. I said it's the mind that continues.

Q. And who is it that keeps this wheel moving?

Lama. Who keeps the wheel of mind moving? Energy. For example, the energy of your mind of yesterday automatically moves your mind of today. It's just like your physical body in that even when your body dies, the energy of its elements continues to run, albeit in another form.

Q. Has there always been the same number of sentient beings? Will there always be the same number?

Lama. In this solar system, the numbers vary. Sometimes more, sometimes less; in this solar system, sentient beings come and go.

Q. Does that mean that we could incarnate into a different solar systems?

Lama. Yes, we incarnate into different worlds. Sometimes we have bodies of form; sometimes our bodies are formless.

But now we have to finish. If you have more questions, please bring them tomorrow night and we can debate together then.

Prince Phillip Theatre, Melbourne University, 4 April 1975

Switzerland, 1978

2

SPIRITUALITY AND MATERIALISM

People often talk about spirituality and materialism, but what do these terms really mean? Actually, this is not a simple subject; it's vast. There are probably countless points of view as to what spirituality and materialism truly are.

On the surface, we might agree, "This is spiritual; that is material," but if you look into it more deeply I think you'll find that as individuals, each of us has a different view.

Some people think that spirituality and materialism are complete opposites—two irreconcilable extremes—and that it's impossible to be spiritual and materialistic at the same time. Others consider that those who seek the spiritual path do so only because they are unhappy with their lives, have failed in the material world and can't find a way to be happy in it, can't face living in normal society and therefore hallucinate that somewhere up there, there's a God in whom they can believe.

Another common misconception is that if you are a spiritual seeker you must abandon all material comfort; that you can't enjoy both together. This kind of superficial contradiction is all too common amongst the people of this Earth—"If it's this, it cannot be that; if it's that, it cannot be this." Should a spiritual practitioner be wealthy, people will say, "How can you be so rich? You're supposed to be spiritual." This kind of philosophical judgment shows a complete lack of understanding of what spiritual and materialistic really are.

My point of view is that all such interpretations are wrong conceptions; too extreme; they are fixed ideas.

Furthermore, there are those who say, "You're a spiritual practitioner? You must be a believer. I don't believe anything." However, a few simple questions will show that they have more beliefs than most religious people. Belief is not simply intellectual. As long as you have attachment to ideas, material things or projections of good and bad, in my view, you're believer. When you say, "I don't believe anything," it's just not true. Belief isn't only the fear that up there in the sky is a God who controls and will punish you. If you really check up on the human mind, you'll never find anyone who believes nothing. It's impossible. As long as people have attachment to anything and ideas of good and bad, as far as I'm concerned, they're believers.

Really wise religious people do not hold extreme beliefs, such as the hallucination that they're under the control of some energy force up there. Therefore, do not think that those who seek the spiritual path are all hallucinating, extreme believers. What they are depends on how they understand the nature of the path they are following.

Of course, I know that some people, especially those brought up in the West, can have a materialistic attitude towards the spiritual path. The moment they hear about Buddhism or some other religion, they are immediately attracted to it. Without understanding the religion or checking that it suits their basic nature, they grasp at it right away: "Oh, this is fantastic." That's extreme. It's also very dangerous. From my point of view, that's not a spiritual attitude. Just because you love some idea doesn't mean that you understand it or that you are able to practice or experience that philosophy. You can label any idea as good, but if it has no influence on your daily life, how can you say, "I love that idea; I'm spiritual." That's ridiculous.

All such attitudes are very dangerous. Spiritual practitioners have to be realistic about their everyday lives instead of hallucinating—"I am Jesus, look at me"; "I am Buddha, look at me"—holding exaggerated views and complete misconceptions of their own reality that have nothing to do with any religion.

Religion is not just some dry, intellectual idea that appeals to you. Rather, it should be your basic philosophy of life; something that through experience you have found relates positively with the energy of your psychological makeup. If you hear an idea that seems to make sense, first see if you can get a taste of it through experience. Only then should you adopt it as your spiritual path.

Say you encounter Buddhist philosophy for the first time: "Oh, fantastic. This is so good." Then, because you regard these new ideas materialistically, you try to make radical changes to your everyday life. You can't do it; it's impossible. You can only change your mind gradually. To actualize Dharma you have to start from where you are and base any practice that you do on that foundation. But to abandon your basic nature and try to change yourself according to some fantastic idea, as if you were changing clothes—that's really hallucinating. That's too extreme. People who do that have no understanding of the nature of the spiritual path. That's dangerous. You check up; we tend to judge things very superficially.

As I said, if we were to ask ourselves what is the nature of spirituality and what is the nature of materialism, we'd all come up with different answers. There would be no unanimous conclusion. This is because we all think differently and we've all had different life experiences. Even if you show a group of people some unknown material substance and ask them to identify it, they do so on the basis of their previous experiences and may come up with many different answers. For similar reasons, we all reply differently when we're asked to define the religious and the materialistic life.

My point of view is that following a spiritual path does not automatically mean that you have to reject material things and leading a materialistic life does not necessarily disqualify you from the spiritual. In fact, even if you are materialistic, if you really check deep within your own mind's nature, you'll find that there's a part of it that is already religious. Even if you declare, "I'm not a believer," nevertheless, within your mind the religious dimension is there. It may not be intellectualized, it may not be your conscious philosophy, but there's a spiritual stream of energy constantly running through your consciousness. Actually, even the intellectual and philosophical aspects of religion are also there in your psyche, but they have not come from books or papers; they have always been there. So be careful. Your extreme views may interpret that spirituality and materialism are completely contradictory, but they are not.

Actually, from the point of view of religious tolerance, the world is now a better place than it was even less than a century ago. At that time people held highly extreme views, especially in the West. Religious practitioners were afraid of non-religious people; non-religious people were afraid of those who were religious. Everybody felt very insecure. This was all based on misconception. Probably most of this is now behind us, but it's possible that some people still feel like this. Certainly, many feel that spiritual and materialistic lives are totally incompatible. It's not true.

Therefore, take the middle way as much as you possibly can. Avoid the extreme of thinking, "I am spiritual"—clinging tightly to that idea, hallucinating by imagining what you think a spiritual life should be—and then neglecting the basic nature of your everyday life—"I'm enjoying my spiritual life so much I don't even want to make tea." Here, there's no harmony between your so-called spiritual life and the demands of your everyday existence. If you really were pursuing a spiritual life, there would be more harmony and better cooperation between the two; instead of a barrier there would be more concern with and understanding of the needs of everyday living. A barrier between the two means there's something wrong with what you're calling your spiritual path; instead of being open to the world around you, you're closed. Therefore, communication is difficult. If the religion you are practicing is a true path and gives satisfactory answers to your dissatisfied mind, you should be better than ever at dealing with your everyday life and living like a decent human being. Living by dry, hallucinated ideas is not realistic; that way, you can't even get breakfast. Check carefully to see what you really understand about your religious practice; you might find much that needs correction.

Everything Lord Buddha said, his entire philosophy and doctrine, was for the purpose of penetrating to the essence of our being, of realizing the nature of the human mind. He never said we just had to believe what he taught. Instead, he encouraged us to try to understand.

Without understanding, your entire spiritual trip is a fantasy, a dream, a hallucination; as soon as someone questions your beliefs, your entire spiritual life collapses like a house of cards. Your hallucinated ideas are like paper, not cement; one question— "What is this?"—and the whole thing disappears. Without understanding, you can't give satisfactory answers about what you are doing.

Therefore, I encourage you to put it all together. Enjoy your material life as much as you can, but at the same time, understand the nature of your enjoyment—the nature of both the object you are enjoying and the mind that is experiencing that enjoyment and how the two relate. If you understand all this deeply, that is religion. If you have no idea of all this, if you see only the outside view and never look to see what is going on inside, your mind is narrow and, from my point of view, materialistic. It is not because you necessarily possess the materials but because of your attitude.

Say I dedicate my life to one object: "This flower is so beautiful. As long as it's alive, my life is worth living. If this flower dies, I want to die too." If I believe this, I'm stupid, aren't I? Of course, the flower is just an example, but such is the extreme view of the materialistic mind. A more realistic approach would be, "Yes, the flower is beautiful, but it won't last. Today it's alive, tomorrow it'll be dead. However, my satisfaction doesn't come from only that flower and I wasn't born human just to enjoy flowers."

Therefore, whatever you understand by religion, Buddhism, or simply philosophical ideas, should be integrated with the basics of your life. Then you can experiment: "Does dissatisfaction come from my own mind or not?" That is enough. You don't need to make extreme radical changes to your life, to suddenly cut yourself off from the world, in order to learn that dissatisfaction comes from your own mind. You can continue to lead a normal life, but at the same time try to observe the nature of the dissatisfied mind. This approach is so realistic, so practical, and in this way you will definitely get all the answers you seek.

Otherwise, if you accept some extreme idea and try to give things up just intellectually, all you do is agitate your life. For the human body to exist you at least should be able to get lunch, or breakfast, or something. Therefore, be realistic. It is not necessary to make radical external changes. You simply have to change internally—stop hallucinating and see reality.

If you really check up, the two extremes—religion and materialism—are equally hallucination; both are projections of a polluted mind making extreme value judgments. Never mind that the person says, "Oh, I don't believe anything...all I believe is that this morning I had breakfast and today I did this and that. What I see and think is real; I don't hallucinate." If you question this person, "What do you think of the color red?" you will automatically reveal that he's hallucinating. He sees the shapes and colors of the sense world but has no idea of their true nature; that they are simply projections of his mind. Ask him, "What color do you like? Do you like black?" "Oh no, I don't like black." "How about white?" "Oh yes, I do like white." So, he likes one thing but not another—two things. That shows his mind is polluted. Anyway, many things in our life experience are not expressed verbally, but they are there, obscured in our minds. It doesn't matter that we don't say the words.

Often we are not sure what we really want. We are too extreme; mentally ill. A fickle thought arises in our mind and we jump at that idea and act upon it. Another idea comes; we jump at that and act some other way. I call that schizophrenic; not checking. Ideas come and go. Instead of grasping at them, check them out. Some people get fixed ideas: "This is absolutely good; that, I hate." Or, somebody says that something is good and you automatically contradict, "No, no, no, no, no." Instead of just rejecting what people say, question why they say it. Try to understand why you don't agree. The more we tie ourselves up with fixed ideas, the more trouble we create for ourselves and others. Somebody changes something—we freak out. Instead of freaking out, check why they're changing that. When you understand their reasons, you won't get so upset. Fixed ideas—

"My life should be exactly like this"—lead only to problems. It's impossible to firmly establish the way your life should be.

Everybody's mind, everybody's basic nature is constantly changing, changing, changing. You have to accept that and bring some flexibility to your ideas of the way things should be. Fixed ideas make life difficult. Why do we solidify ideas: "I want my life to be exactly like this"? Because "I like." That's the reason—because we like things that way. None of us wants to die, but can we fix it so that we won't? We would like to live forever, enjoying life on Earth. Can we fix it so that we will? No, it's impossible. Your basic nature—your mind, your body, the world—is automatically changing. Wanting things to go exactly a certain way is only making trouble for yourself.

When you solidify an idea, you cling to and believe in it. Lord Buddha's psychology teaches us to free ourselves from this kind of grasping—but not to give it up in an emotional, rejecting way, but rather to take the middle way, between the two extremes. If you put your mind wisely into this middle space, there you will find happiness and joy. You don't need to try too hard; automatically, you will discover a peaceful atmosphere, your mind will be balanced and you will dwell in peace and joy.

I think that's enough for now. Perhaps even too much. Anyway, no matter how long we talk, we'll never get through this subject. Therefore, if you have any questions, please ask them. I think that would be better at this point.

Q. What is the benefit of becoming a monk?

Lama. From my point of view, a monk's life offers more flexibility and fewer fixed ideas. If you marry, for example, if you pick one out of all the infinite atoms that exist and dedicate your life to that person, it seems narrow to me. When you become a monk, you dedicate your life to all living beings. Instead of being caught up with just one atom, your mind is more equal. But of course, I'm not saying that this is the only way. If you are wise, you can do anything.

Q. So you are not recommending that everyone go into a monastery?

Lama. It's up to the individual. The world contains so many objects of agitation. If a person's mind is too small and he finds living in the world difficult, perhaps it's better that he go into a monastery. But if a person can live in harmony with the world and, instead of being bothered by the conditions of marriage, can control his mind perfectly and benefit his wife, he can go that route. You can't make a fixed statement; it's an individual thing.

Q. What is enlightenment?

Lama. Simply put, enlightenment is a state beyond the uncontrolled, agitated, dissatisfied mind; a state of perfect freedom, everlasting enjoyment and complete understanding of the nature of the mind.

Q. People talk about seeing light in the mind. What does that mean?

Lama. In general, light is the opposite of darkness, but perhaps I should explain it from the psychological standpoint. When your mind is too narrow, full of grasping ideas, forms, colors and things like that, it tends to be dark and sluggish in nature. When these things disappear, light arises. That's all there is to it. It's just the mind's view. Therefore, don't worry. Actually, you see light every day of your life. Even when it's all dark, you're seeing black light. But whatever light you see—white, black, any color—it's not something that comes from outside of you. It comes from your own mind. It's very important that you investigate this point— whatever light you see comes from your own mind. When someone makes you angry and you see red, that comes from your own mind. It's your own mind's projection; it does not come from some external source. This is interesting. The object of every different mental perception has a color associated with it; each view of the mind is always associated with color. Check up for yourself; experiment with this.

Q. I think I understand what you are saying about visual objects, but what about intellectual concepts like language and grammar—things we are taught at school?

Lama. That also comes from your own mind. Language arises from your natural, inner sound; and without sound, there's no grammar. First there are the vowels—a, e, i, o and u. Without these sounds you cannot make sentences; vowels are put together with consonants and language arises. Grammar is created by the superficial mind; people's minds make language. Any language is the result of people wanting to express certain thoughts that are in their minds and its purpose is communication. Language is actually a symbol for meaning. People want to communicate with each other, so they create language as a means for doing that. But if you grasp too much at language itself, you'll end up with nothingness. Language is produced by the superstitious attitude of attachment to superficial communication. If you want to go beyond superficial communication, you must go beyond ideas, words and grammar. If you think words are the only means of communication, you'll never transcend the superficial view; you'll never understand reality.

Q. Mantras are sound. What is their purpose?

Lama. Actually, mantras are different from ordinary sounds; they help take your mind beyond the superficial view. Our minds are preoccupied with mundane perceptions and split by a constant torrent of thought. If done properly, mantra recitation automatically integrates our minds and creates a calm, peaceful atmosphere within them. It depends on how well you do your recitation. Sometimes you don't reach the level of mental integration; other times you do. However, once you have achieved the perfectly integrated mind of oneness, you no longer need to count or chant mantras. Also, there are different mantras for different purposes. We all have different problems; there's a mantra for every occasion.

Q. I understand that you're saying we should desire

enlightenment, but didn't Lord Buddha say that all desire should be abandoned?

Lama. Well, it's possible to get enlightened without desiring it. The main thing is not to cling too much. If you cling with attachment to the idea of enlightenment, it can become negative instead of positive. You're right. Lord Buddha said not to be attached to even the idea of nirvana or enlightenment. Try to be free, but simply act consciously and correctly with moment to moment awareness of the actions of your body, speech and mind.

Q. You mentioned the animal realm. Once you're an animal, are you stuck there forever? Can animals become enlightened?

Lama. There's no permanent suffering anywhere, including in the animal realm. Animals' lives are also impermanent, constantly changing, changing, changing. Sometimes they change for the good, sometimes for the bad. When they change in a positive direction, that mind can then continue to develop further. In terms of animals attaining enlightenment, they eventually need to be reborn human, but to do that they don't necessarily have to desire enlightenment. If they live in a nice, peaceful environment free of anger and aggression, their minds can gradually develop in such a way that their karma to become human can ripen. But animals that continuously accumulate anger and attachment find their minds becoming more and more confused and they can get reborn in even worse places than the animal realm.

Q. Sometimes when I'm meditating and trying to focus on one object, other objects appear to my mind and distract me. How can I stop that from happening?

Lama. It depends on your ability. If you are trying to concentrate on one thing and something else appears and you can make the distracting object disappear without paying attention to it, that's best, but looking at that object and trying to reject it is no solution. The appearance of such objects is your mind playing tricks on you; they are manifestations of the memory of your old garbage experiences. So instead of rejecting them, what you can do is to penetratingly investigate their nature. When you focus single-pointedly on their nature, the objects disappear—because they come from the mind. Anyway, the mind's view always changes, so distractions are never going to last long.

Thank you. If you have no more questions we can stop here for tonight and I'll see you tomorrow.

Prince Phillip Theatre, Melbourne University, 5 April 1975

3

EXPERIENCING SILENT WISDOM

When your sense perception contacts sense objects and you experience physical pleasure, enjoy that feeling as much as you can. But if the experience of your sense perception's contact with the sense world ties you, if the more you look at the sense world the more difficult it becomes, instead of getting anxious—"I can't control this"—it's better to close your senses off and silently observe the sense perception itself.

Similarly, if you're bound by the problems that ideas create, instead of trying to stop those problems by grasping at some other idea, which is impossible, silently investigate how ideas cause you trouble.

At certain times, a silent mind is very important, but "silent" does not mean closed. The silent mind is an alert, awakened mind; a mind seeking the nature of reality. When problems in the sense world bother you, the difficulty comes from your sense perception, not from the external objects you perceive. And when concepts bother you, that also does not come from outside but from your mind's grasping at concepts. Therefore, instead of trying to stop problems emotionally by grasping at new material objects or ideas, check up silently to see what's happening in your mind.

No matter what sort of mental problem you experience, instead of getting nervous and fearful, sit back, relax, and be as silent as possible. In this way you will automatically be able to see reality and understand the root of the problem.

When we experience problems, either internal or external, our narrow, unskillful mind only makes them worse. When someone with an itchy skin condition scratches it, he feels some temporary relief and thinks his scratching has made it better. In fact, his scratching has made it worse. We're like that; we do the same thing, every day of our lives. Instead of trying to stop problems like this, we should relax and rely on our skillful, silent mind. But silent does not mean dark, non-functioning, sluggish or sleepy.

So now, just close your eyes for five or ten minutes and take a close look at whatever you consider your biggest problem to be.

Shut down your sense perception as much as you possible can, remain completely silent and with introspective knowledge-wisdom, thoroughly investigate your mind.

Where do you hold the idea of "my problem"?

Is it in your brain? In your mouth? Your heart? Your stomach? Where is that idea?

If you can't find the thought of "problem," don't intellectualize; simply relax. If miserable thoughts or bad ideas arise in your mind, just watch how they come, how they go.

Don't react emotionally.

Practicing in this way, you can see how the weak, unskillful mind cannot face problems. But your silent mind of skillful wisdom can face any problem bravely, conquer it and control all your emotional and agitated states of mind.

Don't think that what I'm saying is a Buddhist idea, some Tibetan lama's idea. It can become the actual experience of all living beings throughout the universe.

I could give you many words, many ideas in my lecture tonight, but I think it's more important to share with you the silent experience. That's more realistic than any number of words.

When you investigate your mind thoroughly, you can see clearly that both miserable and ecstatic thoughts come and go. Moreover, when you investigate penetratingly, they disappear altogether. When you are preoccupied with an experience, you think, "I'll never forget this experience," but when you check up skillfully, it automatically disappears. That is the silent wisdom experience. It's very simple, but don't just believe me—experience it for yourself.

In my experience, a silent lecture is worth more than one with many words and no experience. In the silent mind, you find peace, joy and satisfaction.

Silent inner joy is much more lasting than the enjoyment of eating chocolate and cake. That enjoyment is also just a conception.

When you close off your superficial sense perception and investigate your inner nature, you begin to awaken. Why? Because superficial sense perception prevents you from seeing the reality of how discursive thought comes and goes. When you shut down your senses, your mind becomes more conscious and functions better. When your superficial senses are busy, your mind is kind of dark; it's totally preoccupied by the way your senses are interpreting things. Thus, you can't see reality. Therefore, when you are tied by ideas and the sense world, instead of stressing out, stop your sense perception and silently watch your mind. Try to be totally awake instead of obsessed with just one atom. Feel totality instead of particulars.

You can't determine for yourself the way things should be. Things change by their very nature. How can you tie down any idea? You can see that you can't.

When you investigate the way you think—"Why do I say this is good? Why do I say this is bad?"—you start to get real answers as to how your mind really works. You can see how most of your ideas are silly but how your mind makes them important. If you check up properly you can see that these ideas are really nothing. By checking like this, you end up with nothingness in your mind. Let your mind dwell in that state of nothingness. It is so peaceful; so joyful. If you can sit every morning with a silent mind for just ten or twenty minutes, you will enjoy it very much. You'll be able to observe the moment-to-moment movement of your emotions without getting sad.

You will also see the outside world and other people differently; you will never see them as hindrances to your life and they will never make you feel insecure.

Therefore, beauty comes from the mind.

So, that was the experience of silence. But if you have some questions, let's have a question-answer session. You can discuss what I've been saying through your own experience. Observing and investigating your mind is so simple; very simple. Constantly, wherever you go, at any time, you can experience this energy. It's always with you. But chocolate isn't always with you—when you want it, it's not there and when you don't feel like it, there it is in front of you.

The joy of the silent experience comes from your own mind. Therefore, joy is always with you. Whenever you need it, it's always there.

Still, if you have questions, please ask, although an answer from the silent mind is always better than too many words. There are so many views and philosophies; instead of helping, they sometimes cause more confusion. Some English words can mean more than twenty things.

Q. What's the best way to attain enlightenment oneself? Where does one find enlightenment?

Lama. By dealing with your own mind. By knowing your own mind's nature. That's the best thing. Otherwise, you just collect ideas; too many ideas—"This idea; this religion; this religious idea." All you do is collect ideas, but you have no understanding of how they relate to your own mind. Thus, you end up with nothingness. The best thing, the real solution to your own problems, is to face them; to try to understand their nature. If you can do that, problems disappear by themselves. You can discover this through your own personal experience. If you read books containing fantastic ideas, religions and philosophies but don't know how to put those ideas into action, if you don't have the key, the ideas themselves become problems. The best thing you can do is to try to understand your own nature. That's better than trying to find out more about me, for example: "What is this lama?" It's impossible to stop problems that way. But by constantly observing your own everyday life—how your mind interprets your family and friends, how your mind interprets what you feel—by always checking, you will realize that what makes life complicated is your own misconceptions. You will understand that your problems come from you. Now you are starting to learn. The more you understand, the more progress you make, the closer you get to liberation. There's no progress without understanding. That's why Lord Buddha said, all you have to do is understand; then you'll progress along the path. If you have no understanding, even if you learn countless intellectual ideas, they're just ideas; you're wasting your life.

Q. It seems that to achieve the desired result from meditation, you need a certain kind of environment. What are the implications of this fact for those of us who live in a concrete, noisy, nine-to-five world with little or no contact with others interested in the spiritual path. Do you believe that psychedelics like LSD can be important or useful for people like this?

Lama. Well, it's hard to say. I've never taken anything like that. But Buddhist teachings do talk about how material substances affect the human nervous system and the relationship between the nervous system and the mind. We study this kind of thing in Buddhist philosophy. From what I've learned, I would say that taking drugs goes against what Buddhism recommends. However, my own point of view is that people who are completely preoccupied with the sense world, who have no idea of the possibilities of mental development, can possibly benefit from the drug experience. How? If people whose reality is limited to the meat and bone of this human body have this experience, perhaps they'll think, "Wow! I thought this physical world was all there is, but now I can see that it's possible for my mind to develop beyond the constraints of my flesh and blood body." In some cases the drug experience can open up a person's mind to the possibility of mental development. But once you've had that experience, it's wrong to keep taking hallucinogens because the drug experience is not real understanding; it's not a proper realization. The mind is still limited because matter itself is so limited; it's up and down, up and down. Also, if you take too many drugs you can damage your brain. So, that's just my personal point of view.

Q. Do I need anything?

Lama. I hope you need something. No, you definitely need something. But it's for you to check up what you need. Your needs come from within you, not from without. Still, many times we say, "I need this, I need that," and throughout our lives accumulate so much stuff. But when we really check up the why and the how of our needs, we can finish up finding that we need almost nothing.

Q. Are you saying that Western education is a waste of time?

Lama. No, that's not what I'm saying. It depends on the individual; it depends on how you learn, not the education itself. How you learn is what's important.

Q. Could you explain again how we find answers from within ourselves.

Lama. Let your obsessed sense perception rest for a while and allow your silent mind to surface. Then ask your question. You will find that the answer to your question will appear spontaneously from within the peaceful stillness of your silent mind.

Q. Are you saying that we have to enlighten ourselves?

Lama. Yes, that's exactly what I'm saying.

Q. Then why do we need to follow a teacher?

Lama. We need somebody to teach us how to find the answers from within ourselves; how to put our energy into the right channel so that the right answers appear. Most of the time, the answer is here but we're looking for it over there, in completely the opposite direction.

Q. What does Tibetan Buddhism have that other branches of Buddhism do not?

Lama. First, I would say that all branches of Buddhism are teaching fundamentally the same thing—an approach to developing the human mind. But individually, we think, "I'm

Christian, I'm Jewish, I'm this religion, I'm that," but we actually have no idea of how to put our religion into action; we don't know the method. However, that is completely up to the individual. Also, Tibetan Buddhism doesn't contradict the other schools—Zen, Hinayana and so forth. Basically, they are all the same. Of course, we see things from only the outside, so our judgments are very superficial. We ask someone, "What's your religion?" He says, "I'm this…." Then we check to see if the person's happy or not. If we think he's unhappy, we go, "Oh, he's unhappy; that religion must be horrible." Our value judgments are so limited. We should be careful not to do this. For example, tonight I have spoken about many things. If tomorrow someone asks you, "What do you really feel about what Lama said last night?" be careful not to reply as if yours is the definitive view. Everybody here will have a different opinion. We interpret things through our limited point of view, so it can be dangerous to say categorically, "This religion is that; that religion is this."

Q. Well, how do you know whether what you're thinking is right or not?

Lama. Observe carefully. Don't be satisfied with the way your superficial perception interprets things. That's what I keep saying. You have a thousand minds functioning within you. Every minute, every day, they're telling you, "This is good; no, try this; no, maybe this is good…." Many different minds arise: "I want this"; a minute later, "No, I want that." You get so confused. Observe, instead of immediately grasping at whatever your mind fancies the moment it fancies it. Your schizophrenic mind changes its opinion every minute; different ideas keep rushing into your mind; each one generates so much excitement that you grasp at it immediately. That's what gets you into trouble. Therefore, instead of saying, "Oh, fantastic," the moment an idea arises, step back; observe. Check up the why and the how of that idea.

Q. How do you check?

Lama. Deeply; with wisdom. Checking ideas is not like an airport customs inspection. That is so superficial. The checking mind is the penetrative wisdom that sees through to the very heart of all phenomena. Wisdom sees a lot more than just shape and color.

Q. Do you think just by checking within you can find a solution to any problem?

Lama. Sure; if you have enough wisdom. But when you do, you have to make sure that the solution you have found fits the problem. This depends on the nature of the problem, not only on the solution itself. Even if the method is correct, you have to wait for the right time to put it into effect. Timing is very important. If you get emotional—"Oh, there are so many people, so many problems"—and rush about in your car trying to help everybody, you'll finish up creating more problems and having a nervous breakdown.

Q. How is Buddha consciousness lost?

Lama. Buddha hasn't lost his consciousness. Where would it be lost? How could Buddha's consciousness get lost? Buddha hasn't lost anything.

Q. But aren't we in the situation of having lost the enlightenment we once had?

Lama. No, that's a misconception. Once you achieve buddhahood there's no coming down. You remain completely in everlasting satisfaction. It's not like the up and down of the drug experience. When the drug's energy has dissipated, you come down. Enlightenment is not like that; it's completely indestructible, everlasting joy.

Q. With work and family obligations, I find it difficult to maintain my spiritual practice.

Lama. Many people do. The conditions make it difficult. Our baby minds are very susceptible to the environment. An agitated atmosphere agitates our mind. You can observe for yourself the effect different situations have on your mind. But when we attain liberation, or inner freedom, we transcend conditions. When we have reached beyond the conditioned mind, no matter where we are, the external conditions cannot affect us. We're completely in control because we understand the reality of our minds and the environment. Until we do, the conditions are more powerful than our minds and we are easily controlled by the environment.

Q. If one believes that one already has a satisfactory solution to problems, what benefit is there in meditation?

Lama. If someone believes that he has a solution to his problems without meditation—perhaps he's hallucinating. I'm joking. Your question is very important. You have to know what meditation means. Meditation is not just sitting in some corner doing nothing. Meditation means using the wisdom of your intellect and not being satisfied with mere superficial perception. Meditation means seeing beyond the superficial view. That is what we call meditation. Therefore, if one hasn't attained the penetrative wisdom that understands the nature of reality and his entire perception is a hallucination, it's impossible to really solve any problem. He might think he has a solution, but he's dreaming.

Q. Does life start at conception?
Lama. Yes, at conception. Before you come out of your mother's womb—even when you're only a few cells in size—your consciousness is already there. Of course, it's difficult for us to remember this because our minds are so limited, but it's true that our minds and our bodies have been connected from the time of our conception.

Q. What is the best way to control emotions?
Lama. As I've been saying—with the silent mind. When you feel strong emotions arising, instead of getting busy, busy, busy, instead of nervously doing something, relax; try to be silent. There are many ways of doing this. Instead of letting your emotions run wild with your mind, unable to forget whatever it is that's bothering you, sit down, relax, and focus your mind on the flow

of your breath—watch exactly how your breath flows into your nervous system on inhalation and out of it on exhalation. This is very simple. When you concentrate on your breath, you automatically calm down. This is living experience; it has nothing to do with religious belief. You're observing your own nature. As long as you're alive, you're breathing. So, just focus your full attention on the coming and going of your breath and the way you feel. If you can do this, your emotions will automatically settle down and your fixations disappear. It's very simple and very practical. I can guarantee that if you watch your breath for just twenty-one cycles, your nervous emotions will vanish. I'm not making this up or exaggerating. It's people's experience. And to enjoy the benefits of this technique yourself, you don't have to identify with any religious group.

Q. What happens during an initiation?
Lama. Ideally, the mind of the guru and the mind of the disciple merge at the same level. Also, receiving an initiation does not necessitate meeting the guru physically. If you are able to bring your mind up to a certain level, you can initiate yourself. That's possible.

And if there are no further questions, we can stop here. Thank you very much, everybody. Thank you.

Prince Phillip Theatre, Melbourne University, 6 April 1975

Vajrapani Institute, 1983

4

ATTITUDE IS MORE IMPORTANT THAN ACTION

These days, even though many people realize the limitations of material comfort and are interested in following a spiritual path, few really appreciate the true value of practicing Dharma. For most, the practice of Dharma, religion, meditation, yoga, or whatever they call it, is still superficial: they simply change what they wear, what they eat, the way they walk and so forth. None of this has anything to do with the practice of Dharma.

Before you start practicing Dharma, you have to investigate deeply why you are doing it. You have to know exactly what problem you're trying to solve. Adopting a religion or practicing meditation just because your friend is doing it is not a good enough reason.

Changing religions is not like dyeing cloth, like instantly making something white into red. Spiritual life is mental, not physical; it demands a change of mental attitude. If you approach your spiritual practice the way you do material things, you'll never develop wisdom; it will just be an act.

Before setting out on a long journey, you have to plan your course carefully by studying a map; otherwise, you'll get lost. Similarly, blindly following any religion is also very dangerous. In fact, mistakes on the spiritual path are much worse than those made in the material world. If you do not understand the nature of the path to liberation and practice incorrectly, you'll not only get nowhere but will finish up going in the opposite direction.

Therefore, before you start practicing Dharma, you have to know where you are, your present situation, the characteristic nature of your body, speech and mind. Then you can see the necessity for practicing Dharma, the logical reason for doing it; you can see your goal more clearly, with your own experience. If you set out without a clear vision of what you are doing and where you're trying to go, how can you tell if you're on the right path? How can you tell if you've gone wrong? It's a mistake to act blindly, thinking, "Well, let me do something and see what happens." That's a recipe for disaster.

Buddhism is less interested in what you do than why you do it—your motivation. The mental attitude behind an action is much more important than the action itself. You might appear to outside observers as humble, spiritual and sincere, but if what's pushing you from within is an impure mind, if you're acting out of ignorance of the nature of the path, all your so-called spiritual efforts will lead you nowhere and will be a complete waste of time.

Often your actions look religious but when you check your motivation, the mental attitude that underlies them, you find that they're the opposite of what they appear. Without checking, you can never be sure if what you're doing is Dharma or not.

You might go to church on Sundays or to your Dharma center every week, but are these Dharma actions or not? This is what you have to check. Look within and determine what kind of mind is motivating you to do these things.

Many countries have their own historical religious cultures, but it's a misconception to think that simply following these customs makes your actions spiritual. First of all, what is culture, what is social custom? Societal conventions have nothing to do with universal understanding-knowledge-wisdom. And at an individual level, it doesn't matter where you come from—East or West—your society's traditions of eating, drinking, sleeping and other worldly activities have nothing to do with religion.

If you think they do, your understanding is really primitive. I don't mean your religion is primitive; I mean your understanding of your religion is primitive—whether you're Buddhist, Hindu, Christian or anything else, your view of your religion is a total misconception. If you go to your church or temple simply out of custom—"I go because everybody else does"—it's silly and illogical. There's no significance. You don't know what you're doing or why.

If you are going to practice Dharma, meditate, follow the spiritual path, do so with understanding. If you don't understand what you're doing or why, don't do it.

For example, when Lord Buddha formulated the rules of monastic conduct, the vinaya, he said, "If your motivation for becoming a monk or nun is simply to get food, clothing and shelter, you can't be ordained." Look at why you became a member of your own religion in the light of what the Buddha said.

Often we adopt one faith or another for temporal reasons of reputation or comfort, or because "I like their ideas." How do you know that you like their ideas? What is it about them that you like? Have you really checked them out? Have you checked to see if those ideas fit your everyday life? Will they bring you spiritual realizations and an everlastingly peaceful mind? Or do they just sound good? "I like their ideas; they sound good." How do they sound good? You have to check up.

Our grasping, superficial mind is always just looking outside. We never look to see how the ideas we hear suit our daily life. That's why there's always a big gap between us—the human beings—and the theory and practice of religion. Then, what's the purpose of that path? It's completely useless. Our ego is still immersed in its materialistic trip. Some people join a spiritual community because, "It's so easy. They give me great food and I don't need to work." That's so small-minded. Still, many people are like that. I'm not criticizing anybody in particular; I'm just generalizing. This is just a simple example. You'll find people like that in every religion.

Therefore, when you decide to practice any religion, you have to know why. It's not simply a matter of learning what that religion says. You have to check with your own mind, "Why do I accept this religion's ideas?" That's what you need to check. Otherwise, you can study your religion's philosophy in depth and have a head full of beautiful ideas but still have no clue how those ideas relate to your life. That's a total misconception of the purpose of religion.

If you think practicing religion means simply learning new ideas, you'd be better off sucking a piece of candy. At least you'd get a little satisfaction; you'd alleviate your thirst for a few moments. If you spend months and years studying new ideas, collecting information, you're wasting your time; it all becomes garbage. I'm not criticizing religion here; I'm criticizing your primitive mind.

Now, you might be thinking, "This lama is from Tibet. He's the primitive one. He must be joking, calling me primitive." Well, you might be highly competent when it comes to conducting your modern, twentieth century life, but in terms of spiritual psychology, perhaps you really are primitive. It's possible. In the industrialized world, it's very difficult to live in the experience of the teachings. The materialistic vibration of worldly objects is far too strong.

It's possible that from the time you embarked on your spiritual journey up to the now, you've gotten nowhere, that you're not the slightest bit spiritual. You check up. If your spiritual journey has been one of simply grasping at intellectual ideas, you've definitely gotten nowhere, you're not at all religious—even though you claim to be a follower of this religion or that. If that indeed is what you declare, check up why you say it.

It's very interesting to check different people's ideas of what constitutes religious practice. Each individual has his or her own personal opinion. There's no consensus. People's limited minds have a limited view of religion and its value. Therefore, they say, "This religion is fanatical; this religion is that; that religion is this...." You can't say that. It's not the religion; it's the opinion of the followers.

When we say, "This religion has degenerated," what we actually mean is that we have degenerated; we lack knowledge wisdom. We say, "This religion used to be like this; now it has degenerated," but it's we who have degenerated. You can't say the religion has degenerated. Religion is knowledge-wisdom. How can knowledge-wisdom degenerate?

Still, you're going to say, "I practice religion; I meditate. I do this; I do that. I pray; I read Dharma books." Anybody can say, "I practice this, I practice that," but how does what you say you do relate to your mind? That's what you have to check. Does your practice solve your mental problems and bring perfect realizations and universal knowledge-wisdom? If your answer is "Yes," then OK.

It's strange but true that often, once we have accepted a certain religious point of view, we become complete fanatics: "This is the only way. All other paths are wrong." However, this doesn't mean that our religion is a fanatical religion; it simply means that we've become religious fanatics. Our minds close up and all we can see is our own narrow view. Therefore, we say, "This is that." But even within Buddhism, there are many different ways to practice. Religious practice is a highly individualized thing.

Actually, according to the usual Western understanding of what constitutes religion, Buddhism shouldn't be considered to be one. Most people have a fairly fixed idea of what religion is, and according to this, Buddhism doesn't fit. Of course, Buddhism has its religious aspects, but it also has philosophical, psychological, scientific, logical and many other characteristics. Also, Lord Buddha gave many different levels of teaching, according to the various levels of mind of his many students. He himself said that sometimes his teachings appear to be contradictory. "I tell some students, 'This is like this'; I tell others, 'This is like that.' It depends on what each individual needs. Therefore, I never want my followers to say, 'This is correct because the Buddha said so.' That's totally wrong."

You have to check up. It's your responsibility to know whether something is right or wrong. You can't just say, "This is true because Buddha said, because God said." Lord Buddha himself made that very clear.

He explained, "I teach the same thing differently because people's minds are different. Since one explanation doesn't fit all, I present my teachings in a graded, systematic order." For example, while the Buddha taught more advanced students that there is no soul, he taught simpler ones that there was one. Why did he give such contradictory teachings? It was in order to prevent beginners from falling into a nihilistic extreme. Later on, when they were ready, he would also teach them that actually, there's no such thing as a permanent, self-existent soul.

The conclusion is that Lord Buddha taught according to people's individual psychology. Every teaching should be taken personally. If you look at the way Buddhism is practiced in different countries, you'll see that each one has its own particular practices, but you can't judge all of Buddhism by the practices of one individual group. For example, Tibetan Buddhists offer a lot of incense and butter lamps. Just looking at that might lead you to believe that these are essential practices and that there's no way to practice without offering these things. But Tibet's great yogi Milarepa lived in the mountains without food or clothes, let alone incense and butter lamps, and he was certainly able to practice.

Therefore, the way to practice religion is not according to

custom or through simply superficial change. It is entirely to do with your psychological attitude of mind.

There's a Tibetan story that illustrates this point. Once, a famous yogi called Dromtönpa saw a man circumambulating a stupa, and said to him, "Circumambulating stupas is all well and good, but wouldn't it be better if you practiced Dharma?" and walked off.

The man was a little puzzled and thought, "Perhaps he means that circumambulating stupas is too simple a practice for me and that I'd be better off studying texts."

Some time later, Dromtönpa saw him reading holy books very intently and said, "Studying texts is all well and good, but wouldn't it be better if you practiced Dharma?" and again walked off.

The man was a little more puzzled and thought, "What, again? There must be something wrong with me." So he asked around, "What kind of practice does the yogi Dromtönpa do?" Then he realized, "He meditates. He must mean I should meditate."

Some time later, Dromtönpa ran into him again, and asked, "What are you up to these days?" The man said, "I've been doing a lot of meditation."

Then Dromtönpa said to him, "Meditation is all well and good, but wouldn't it be better if you practiced Dharma?"

Now the man was completely exasperated and snapped, "Practice Dharma! Practice Dharma! What do you mean, 'Practice Dharma'?"

Then the great yogi Dromtönpa replied, "Turn your mind away from attachment to the worldly life."

You can circumambulate holy objects, go to churches,

monasteries and temples, meditate in some corner doing nothing, but, Dromtönpa was saying, if you don't change your mental attitude, your old habits of attachment and grasping at objects of the senses, no matter what you do, you won't find peace of mind; your practices will be ineffective. If you don't change your mind, no matter how many external changes you make, you'll never progress along the spiritual path; the causes of agitation will remain within you.

These days, many people are interested in meditation, and, of course, many people benefit from their practice. Nevertheless, if you don't change the basic agitated nature of your mind and just think, arrogantly, "I'm meditating," there'll always be something wrong with your meditation. Don't think that meditation is always right, no matter how you do it. It's an individual thing, and whether it benefits you or not depends upon what you understand and the way in which you practice.

However, if besides just knowing the theory, the dry ideas, of your spiritual path, you put what you know into action in your daily life as sincerely as you can, your practice of Dharma, religion, meditation or whatever you want to call it will be fantastically useful; very powerful. If, on the other hand, you have some kind of fixed idea that has nothing whatsoever to do with the truth—"This is religion"—you'll be running as fast as you can in the opposite direction, your mind still polluted by thoughts of "I am this, I am that." You must check up. It's very dangerous.

Therefore, Lord Buddha said that weak-minded people who lack the confidence to face life and turn to religion grasping for a way to make their lives easier are disqualified from becoming monks or nuns. He was very clear about this; he pointed directly at the mind. It's the same for us: if we join a religious community in order to earn a living, enhance our reputation or find other material benefits, we're dreaming; it's completely unrealistic. This is never the way to satisfaction. If we have that kind of inferior, spiritually primitive mind, we'll never solve our problems or gain higher realizations. It's impossible.

Therefore, as I said at the outset, Buddhism isn't interested in the actions you perform or your external aspect but in your state of mind. It's your psychological mental attitude that determines whether your actions become the path to inner realization and liberation or the cause of suffering and confusion.

Lord Buddha said, "Don't be attached to my philosophy and doctrine. Attachment to any religion is simply another form of mental illness."

We see people all over Earth fighting each other in the name of religion, waging war, seizing territory and killing each other. All such actions are so totally misconceived. Religion is not land; religion is not property. People are so ignorant. How can any of this help? Religion is supposed to bring inner peace and a better life, but instead, people use it to create only more confusion and anger. None of this has anything to do with any religion, not only Buddhism.

Dharma practice is a method for totally releasing attachment. But be careful. You may say, "I'm not interested in material development any more; it's wrong" but then sublimate all your materialistic desires into your religion. Instead of eradicating your deeply rooted attachment, you channel it into something more acceptable. But it's still the same old trip. You see that possessions don't bring happiness but then grasp at your religion instead. Then, when somebody says, "Your religion is rubbish," you freak out.

Another Tibetan story shows the lack of connection between intellectual knowledge and ingrained habit. A monk once asked one of his friends, "What are you up to these days?" and the friend replied, "I've been doing a lot of meditation on patience."

Then the monk said, "Well, big patience meditator, eat shit!"

His friend immediately got upset and retorted angrily, "You eat shit yourself!"

This shows how we are. Meditation on patience is supposed to stop anger, but when the monk tested his friend, the meditator got upset at the slightest provocation. He hadn't integrated the idea of patience with his mind. Then, what's the point? It's like you spend your whole life making warm clothes; more and more clothes. Then one day you're out, get caught in a blizzard and freeze to death. This kind of thing is common. We've all heard of millionaires who die of hunger. So, in that last story, the meditator put all his energy into his practice in order to release anger and attachment, but when confronted with a real life situation, he could not control his mind.

If you really, sincerely practice religion with understanding, you will find complete freedom, and when you encounter problems, you'll have no trouble at all. This sort of experience shows that you've reached your goal; that you have really put your knowledge-wisdom into action.

When we're happy, superficially happy, we talk about religion with much energy—"This is great, so good, blah, blah, blah"—discussing all kinds of ideas with great enthusiasm, but the moment something horrible happens, the moment we encounter difficulty, we've got nothing. Our mind is completely empty: no understanding, no wisdom, no control. This sort of experience shows how utterly primitive our understanding of religion, Buddhism, Dharma, meditation or whatever you call it really is.

If you have right understanding and put yourself onto the right path with the right mental attitude, there's no doubt that you'll be able to put a definite end to all psychological problems. Therefore, if you want to be a true practitioner of religion, a proper meditator, instead of hallucinating with a mind polluted by theory and ideas, try to develop a clean, clear, realistic understanding and act gradually in the path to liberation. If you do, realizations will definitely come.

If a starving person suddenly gorges himself on rich food, he'll send his stomach into shock. Instead of benefiting, he'll just destroy himself. Rather than checking to see what's best at that particular moment, he just takes the idea "rich food is good for you" and stuffs himself with the best food available. Just because food is good doesn't mean it's good for you. It depends on the individual.

Similarly, before you launch into all kinds of spiritual practice, you need to check what's appropriate for you in your present situation. You need to be aware of your mental problems and lifestyle, examine the many different methods that exist, and then make a conscious decision based on your current situation and what approach suits you at the time. Before you engage in any practice, check to see if it's really right for you or not.

Practices aren't good or bad in themselves. A method that's fantastically good for one person can be poison for another. Something can sound great in theory but turn into poison upon contact with your nervous system; your body, speech and mind.

If you understand your own mind, you can definitely put it into the right space and gain control over it. With understanding, it's easy. But if you don't understand the key, you can't force it. Control has to come naturally. There's no such thing as instant mental control.

Therefore, my conclusion is that right mental attitude is much more important than action. Don't bring your materialistic way of life to your Dharma practice. It doesn't work. Before meditating, check and correct your motivation. If you do this, your meditation will become much easier and more worthwhile, and your right action will bring realizations. You don't need to be hungry for realizations, grasping, "Oh, if I do this, will I get some fantastic realizations?" You don't need expectation; realizations will come automatically. Once you've set your mind on the right path, realizations will come of their own accord.

Nor should you grasp at your faith such that if somebody says, "You're religion is bad," you angrily turn upon that person. That is totally unrealistic. The purpose of religion is to free you from the agitated, uncontrolled mind. Therefore, if somebody says your religion is bad, why get angry? You should be trying to let go of that kind of mind as much as you possibly can. When you release the deluded mind, inner peace, realizations, nirvana, God, Buddha, Dharma and Sangha—whatever you want to call it, there are so many names—will automatically be there. It's a natural thing.

Some people think, "I love religion. It has so many wonderful ideas." You love the ideas but if you never relate your religion's teachings to your mind, never put them into action, what's the point? You'd be better off with fewer ideas. Too many ideas create conflict within your mind and give you a headache. If all you're interested in is religious ideas, if you're all hung up on ideas up there while your life's going on down here, there's a big gap between your body, speech and mind down here on Earth and your big ideas up in the sky. Then, because of the gap, the two things start to bother you: "Oh, now religion's not so good. My head hurts. I thought religion was fantastic, but now it's causing me more trouble." All you can do is complain. But the problem comes from you. Instead of putting two things together, religion and your life, you've created a split.

That's why Lord Buddha called the dualistic mind negative; it always causes mental disturbance. It makes you fight yourself. The mind that reaches beyond duality becomes the buddha mind, ultimate wisdom, absolute consciousness, perfect peace, universal consciousness—there are many things that you can call it.

You can see how your dualistic mind functions in your daily life. Whenever you find something you like, you automatically start looking around to see if there's anything better. There's always conflict in your mind: "This is nice, but what about that?" The advertising industry is built on exploiting this universal human tendency and the world of material development has grown exponentially because one mind is always competing with another.

However, that's all I have to say right now, but if you have any questions, please ask.

Q. When I check, I see that things are coming from emotions like greed or fear, but what can I do about it? I know where they're coming from but they still keep coming. How should I handle that?

Lama. That's a good question. The thing is that you see the superficial emotion but you don't really see where it's coming from, the energy that causes it to arise. You don't see the deep origin of that emotion. It's like you're looking at a flower but you can't see its root. You say that you know where the emotions are coming from but actually you don't. If you really understood the root of problems they would disappear of their own accord.

However, when you're in a situation where you're psychologically bothered the way that you describe, instead of obsessing over how you feel, focus instead on how the bothered mind arises. If you check up properly with introspective knowledge-wisdom, that troubled mind will disappear by itself. You don't need to drive it away by force. Just watch. Be wise and relaxed. Yours is a good question; many people have that experience. Deal with it by paying less attention to the superficial emotion and whatever sense object might have precipitated it and looking instead deep into your mind to determine what's really making that emotion arise.

Theosophical Society, Adyar Theatre, Sydney, 7 April 1975

Lake Arrowhead, California, July 1975

5

AN INTRODUCTION TO MEDITATION

From the beginning of human evolution on this planet, people have tried their best to be happy and enjoy life. During this time, they have developed an incredible number of different methods in pursuit of these goals. Among these methods we find different interests, different jobs, different technologies and different religions. From the manufacture of the tiniest piece of candy to the most sophisticated spaceship, the underlying motivation is to find happiness. People don't do these things for nothing. Anyway, we're all familiar with the course of human history; beneath it all is the constant pursuit of happiness.

However—and Buddhist philosophy is extremely clear on this—no matter how much progress you make in material development, you'll never find lasting happiness and satisfaction; it's impossible. Lord Buddha stated this quite categorically. It's impossible to find happiness and satisfaction through material means alone.

When Lord Buddha made this statement, he wasn't just putting out some kind of theory as an intellectual skeptic. He had learned this through his own experience. He tried it all: "Maybe this will make me happy; maybe that will make me happy; maybe this other thing will make me happy." He tried it all, came to a conclusion and then outlined his philosophy. None of his teachings are dry, intellectual theories.

Of course, we know that modern technological advances can solve physical problems, like broken bones and bodily pain. Lord Buddha would never say these methods are ridiculous, that we don't need doctors or medicine. He was never extreme in that way.

However, any sensation that we feel, painful or pleasurable, is extremely transitory. We know this through our own experience; it's not just theory. We've been experiencing the ups and downs of physical existence ever since we were born. Sometimes we're weak; sometimes we're strong. It always changes. But while modern medicine can definitely help alleviate physical ailments, it will never be able to cure the dissatisfied, undisciplined mind. No medicine known can bring satisfaction.

Physical matter is impermanent in nature. It's transitory; it never lasts. Therefore, trying to feed desire and satisfy the dissatisfied mind with something that's constantly changing is hopeless, impossible. There's no way to satisfy the uncontrolled, undisciplined mind through material means.

In order to do this, we need meditation. Meditation is the right medicine for the uncontrolled, undisciplined mind. Meditation is the way to perfect satisfaction. The uncontrolled mind is by nature sick; dissatisfaction is a form of mental illness. What's the right antidote to that? It's knowledge-wisdom; understanding the nature of psychological phenomena; knowing how the internal world functions. Many people understand how machinery operates but they have no idea about the mind; very few people understand how their psychological world works. Knowledge-wisdom is the medicine that brings that understanding.

Every religion promotes the morality of not stealing, not telling lies and so forth. Fundamentally, most religions try to lead their followers to lasting satisfaction. What is the Buddhist approach to stopping this kind of uncontrolled behavior? Buddhism doesn't just tell you that engaging in negative actions is bad; Buddhism explains how and why it's bad for you to do such things. Just telling you something's bad doesn't stop you from doing it. It's still just an idea. You have to put those ideas into action.

How do you put religious ideas into action? If there were no method for putting ideas into action, no understanding of how the mind works, you might think, "It's bad to do these things; I'm a bad person," but you still wouldn't be able to control yourself; you wouldn't be able to stop yourself from doing negative actions. You can't control your mind simply by saying, "I want to control my mind." That's impossible. But there is a psychologically effective method for actualizing ideas. It's meditation.

The most important thing about religion is not the theory, the good ideas. They don't bring much change into your life. What you need to know is how to relate those ideas to your life, how to put them into action. The key to this is knowledge-wisdom. With knowledge-wisdom, change comes naturally; you don't have to squeeze, push or pump yourself. The undisciplined, uncontrolled mind comes naturally; therefore, so should its antidote, control.

As I said, if you live in an industrialized society, you know how mechanical things operate. But if you try to apply that knowledge to your spiritual practice and make radical changes to your mind and behavior, you'll get into trouble. You can't change your mind as quickly as you can material things.

When you meditate, you make a penetrative investigation into the nature of your own psyche to understand the phenomena of your internal world. By gradually developing your meditation technique, you become more and more familiar with how your mind works, the nature of dissatisfaction and so forth and begin to be able to solve your own problems.

For example, just to keep your house neat and tidy, you need to discipline your actions to a certain extent. Similarly, since the dissatisfied mind is by nature disorderly, you need a certain degree of understanding and discipline to straighten it out. This is where meditation comes in. It helps you understand your mind and put it in order.

But meditation doesn't mean just sitting in some corner doing nothing. There are two types of meditation, analytical and concentrative. The first entails psychological self-observation, the second developing single-pointed concentration.

Perhaps you're going to say, "Concentration? I don't have any concentration," but that's not true. Without concentration, you couldn't survive for even a day; you couldn't even drive a car. Every human mind has at least a superficial degree of concentration. But developing that to its infinite potential takes meditation—a great deal of meditation. Therefore, we all have to work on the concentration we already have.

Of course, when you lose control of your mind, when you get angry or overwhelmed by some other emotion, you lose even the little concentration that you do have, but still, single-pointed concentration is not something that does not exist within you. It is not impossible to attain, beyond reach, way up in the sky with no connection to you. You don't have to approach concentration from a long way off. It's not like that. You already have some concentration; it just needs to be developed. Then you can straighten out your disorderly, dualistic mind. The dualistic mind is not integrated. As long as it remains that way, it remains dissatisfied by nature, and even though you think you are physically and mentally healthy, you're mentally ill.

We tend to interpret dissatisfaction extremely superficially. We say, glibly, "I'm never satisfied" but we don't really understand what dissatisfaction is or how deep it runs. Someone suggests, "You're dissatisfied because you didn't get enough milk from your mother," and we think, "Oh, yes, that's probably why." This kind of explanation of mental problems is totally off the mark; a complete misconception. Also, dissatisfaction does not come from only inborn, internal sources. It can also come from philosophy or doctrine.

Wherever it comes from, dissatisfaction is a deep psychological problem and not necessarily something that you're consciously aware of. You think you're healthy, but then why can a small change in your conditions cause you to totally freak out? It's because the seed of problems lies deep in your subconscious. You're not free of problems; you're just unaware of what's in your mind. This is a very dangerous situation to be in.

Analytical meditation, checking your own mind, is not something that demands strong faith. You don't need to believe in anything. Just put it into practice and experience it with your own mind. It is an extremely scientific process. Lord Buddha taught that it's possible for all people to reach the same level of view—not materially but internally, in terms of spiritual realization. Through meditation, we can all attain the same goal by realizing the ultimate nature of our mind.

We often find that people fear those from different countries or religions; they're suspicious, insecure: "I'm not sure about him." This happens because we don't understand each other. If we really understood and communicated with each other, our fears would disappear. Our understanding of what other religions teach and how they affect human development is very limited; therefore, we feel insecure when interacting with their followers.

We don't think anything of a big restaurant having an extensive menu. Different people like different kinds of food in order to enjoy their lives and feel satisfied. It's the same thing with religion. Different paths are necessary for different people's minds. If you understand this, you won't feel uncomfortable with practitioners of other religions; you'll accept them as they are.

Our problem is that we don't accept ourselves as we are and we don't accept others as they are. We want things to be other than they are because we don't understand the nature of reality. Our superficial view, fixed ideas and wrong conceptions prevent us from seeing the reality of what we are and how we exist.

Through meditation, you can discover how even actions of body and speech are uncontrollably psychologically motivated. This discovery leads you to natural control of all your actions. An understanding of your psychological impulses is all you need to become your own psychologist. Then you don't need to run to others like a baby, "Am I all right? Do you think I'm OK?" It's babyish to always be asking somebody else if you're OK. It makes your whole life baby-like and you always feel insecure. Having to rely on somebody else to tell you you're OK only makes your life more difficult. Anyway, half the time you're not going to believe what the other person says, so why bother? It all becomes a ridiculous joke.

You should know every aspect your own life. Your life will be more integrated and you'll see things more clearly. A partial view of life can only make you insecure.

There are many types of psychological impulse driving you to do what you do. Some of these are positive, others negative. Instead of simply doing whatever your impulses dictate, it's better to step back and ask, "Why?"

For example, when you have a headache, instead of asking yourself, "What is this headache?" ask, "Why do I have a headache? Where has it come from?" Investigating the source of the headache is more interesting than simply trying to find out what it is. Sometimes just understanding its source can make it go away. Just wondering what it is can never lead to understanding. All you see is the superficial feeling, not its background or deep root.

Sometimes people think, "I'm getting older every day. How is it possible to develop the mind?" If you think that your mind ages and degenerates the way your body does, you're wrong. The way the mind and body function and develop is different.

Meditation isn't necessarily some kind of holy activity; when you meditate, you don't have to imagine holy things up there in the sky. Simply examining your life from the time you were born up till now—looking at the kind of trip you've been on and what sort of psychological impulses have been propelling you—is meditation. Observing your mind is much more interesting than watching TV. Once you've seen your mind, you'll find television boring. Checking in detail what you've been doing from the time you were born—not so much your physical actions but the psychological impulses driving you to do them—is extremely interesting and is how to become familiar with the way your internal world functions.

Analyzing your own mind with your own knowledge-wisdom makes you mentally healthy. It's how you discover that your enjoyment does not depend on chocolate; you can be happy and satisfied without chocolate. Normally you tend to believe, "As long as I have chocolate, I'll be happy. I can't be happy without it." You make your own philosophy of life with this kind of determination, which comes from attachment. Then, when the chocolate disappears, you get nervous: "Oh, now I'm unhappy." But it's not the absence of chocolate that's making you unhappy; it's your fixed ideas. It's the way your mind tricks you into believing that your happiness depends on external objects. It's your psychological impulses that make you mentally ill. People get homesick, don't they? Well, here's a new type of illness: choc-sick. I hope you get what I'm saying.

Of course, this is just one example of how our mind gets fixed ideas. In our lifetime, we fixate on thousands of ideas in this way: "If I have this, I'll be happy; if I have that, I'll be happy. I can't be happy if I don't have this; I can't be happy if I don't have that." We fixate on this, we fixate on that, but life is constantly changing, running like an automatic watch. You can see impermanence simply through observation.

Fixed ideas shake us; they make our mind uncomfortable, agitated and split. According to Lord Buddha, putting strong faith in material objects, thinking, "only this will make me happy," is a total fantasy.

When you understand your relationship with chocolate, you know it's impermanent. Chocolate comes; chocolate goes; chocolate disappears. That's natural. When you understand it's natural, you have no fear. Otherwise, your clinging to chocolate is a rejection of the natural order. How can you reject the world? "I want to remain sixteen forever." No matter how much you wish for things to stay the same, you're asking the impossible. It's a complete misconception. From the Buddhist point of view, you're dreaming. Irrespective of whether you have faith in religion or reject it, you're dreaming.

If you have the psychological tendency to reify ideas, you're a believer. Even though you say, proudly, "I'm a skeptic; I don't believe anything," it's not true. Check up: you're a believer. Just two or three questions will prove that. Do you think some things are good? Do you think some things are bad? Of course you do. Those are beliefs. Otherwise, what is belief?

A belief is something you create with your own logic—irrespective of whether it's right or wrong. Everybody has some reason for thinking, "This is good; that is bad." Even if it's completely illogical, it's reason enough for some people to conclude, "Wow! I like that." Because of this, because of that, they think, "Yes." That's the fixed idea; that's the belief.

I'm not just being cynical. This is my own experience. I have met many skeptical Westerners and checked. Intellectually, they say, "I don't believe anything," but ask them a couple of questions and you'll immediately expose many beliefs within them. This is living experience, not some abstract philosophy.

However, the function of meditation is to reintegrate the split mind; to make the fragmented mind whole. Meditation brings satisfaction to the dissatisfied mind and explodes the idea, or belief, that happiness depends on circumstances alone.

It is important to know this. Weak people can't face problems. Meditation is a way of helping you become strong enough to face your problems instead of running away from them. It allows you to face and deal with your problems skillfully.

According to Lord Buddha's philosophy and the experience of generations of Buddhist practitioners, you can't stop problems simply because somebody says, "You have this problem because of this, that or the other." Somebody interprets something for you, says a few words, and all of a sudden you see the light, "Oh, yes, thank you; my problem's solved." That's impossible. The root of problems is much too deep for something like that to work. That's too superficial an approach to eradicate problems.

The root of problems is not intellectual. If it were, if problems came simply from ideas, then perhaps somebody's suggesting to you that if you changed your way of thinking all your problems would be solved could work. However, to overcome the dissatisfied, undisciplined mind and put an end to psychological problems, you need to become the psychologist. In other words, you need to become knowledge-wisdom.

To liberate yourself, you must know yourself, and getting to know yourself is a fantastic achievement. Then, no matter where you go—up in the sky, under the earth—you will carry the solution to your problems with you.

Chocolate, on the other hand, cannot always be with you. Anyway, you know from your own experience that no matter where you go, as long as you bring your dissatisfied mind along with you, you're always unhappy. The place is not the problem. It's your mind. Even if you go to the moon, you can't escape your problems. Your dissatisfied mind is still there. What, then, is the point of going to the moon if you bring your dissatisfied mind along? We think, "Wow! The moon! Fantastic!" It's not fantastic; it's just another trip.

If you check more deeply, you'll find that whatever you normally think of as fantastic—sense pleasures and so forth—is not at all fantastic. You're just running around in circles; it's the same old trip, over and over again. Your mind changes, you think, "I'm happy," you get bored, you change again, and so it goes, and the little happiness that you do experience never lasts. To experience everlasting satisfaction, freedom and enjoyment, you must bring your own wisdom into play and try to be totally conscious and aware of your own behavior and the impulses that drive you to act, your motivation for doing what you do.

If you do that, you'll make your powerful, precious human life really worthwhile. If you don't, well, it's uncertain whether your life will be worthwhile or not.

Isn't this simple? How difficult is it to check your mind? You don't have to go to a temple; you don't have to go to church. Anyway, your mind is your temple; your mind is your church. This is where you integrate your mind through your own knowledge-wisdom. It's very simple. And you can't reject what I'm saying: "I don't need to understand my own psychological impulses." You can't say that. It's your own mind we're talking about. You have to know your own psychological phenomena. They're part of you; you have to know who you are, your own nature. Lord Buddha never stressed, "You have to know Buddha." His emphasis was, "You have to know yourself."

Usually we understand observing our own behavior to mean watching what we do physically, but psychological impulses do not necessarily translate into overt action. To observe those impulses that do not manifest externally and are therefore obscured from view, we need to meditate. When we meditate deeply, we integrate, or unify, our mind, thereby automatically controlling the agitation that normally arises from the dualistic view projected by our sense perception. In other words, we are able to transcend our sense perception. We can all reach this level.

Therefore, check your own potential to understand your psychological impulses and develop everlasting satisfaction and joy. By checking, you can reach conclusions; without checking, you never reach any conclusion and your whole life becomes wishy-washy, uncertain and insecure.

Why are we not at peace? Because we're not satisfied. From the Buddhist point of view, the dissatisfied mind is the culprit; the real problem. The nature of dissatisfaction is agitation; it functions to disturb our peace of mind.

By analyzing material things in great detail, people discover where they come from and what they're made of. If you put this kind of effort into investigating your internal world, you'll be able to find true satisfaction.

Perhaps that's enough, and since you don't have any questions, I'll simply say good night and thank you very much.

Anzac House, Sydney, 8 April 1975

Switzerland, 1978

6

FOLLOW YOUR PATH WITHOUT ATTACHMENT

Those who practice meditation or religion should not cling with attachment to any idea.

Fixed ideas are not external phenomena. Our minds often grasp at things that sound good, but this can be extremely dangerous. We too easily accept things we hear as good: "Oh, meditation is very good." Of course, meditation is good if you understand what it is and practice it correctly; you can definitely find answers to life's questions. What I'm saying is that whatever you do in the realm of philosophy, doctrine or religion, don't cling to the ideas; don't be attached to your path.

Again, I'm not talking about external objects; I'm talking about inner, psychological phenomena. I'm talking about developing a healthy mind, developing what Buddhism calls indestructible understanding-wisdom.

Some people enjoy their meditation and the satisfaction it brings but at the same time cling strongly to the intellectual idea of it: "Oh, meditation is so perfect for me. It's the best thing in the world. I'm getting results. I'm so happy!" But how do they react if somebody puts their practice down? If they don't get upset, that's fantastic. It shows that they are doing their religious or meditation practice properly.

Similarly, you might have tremendous devotion to God or Buddha or something based on deep understanding and great experience and be one hundred percent sure of what you're doing, but if you have even slight attachment to your ideas, if someone says, "You're devoted to Buddha? Buddha's a pig!" or "You believe in God? God's worse than a dog!" you're going to completely freak out. Words can't make Buddha a pig or God a dog, but still, your attachment, your idealistic mind totally freaks: "Oh, I'm so hurt! How dare you say things like that?"

No matter what anybody says—Buddha is good, Buddha is bad—the absolutely indestructible characteristic nature of the Buddha remains untouched. Nobody can enhance or decrease its value. It's exactly the same when people tell you you're good or bad; irrespective of what they say, you remain the same. Others' words can't change your reality. Therefore, why do you go up and down when people praise or criticize you? It's because of your attachment; your clinging mind; your fixed ideas. Make sure you're clear about this.

Check up. It's very interesting. Check your psychology. How do you respond if somebody tells you your whole path is wrong? If you truly understand the nature of your mind, you will never react to that kind of thing, but if you don't understand your own psychology, if you hallucinate and are easily hurt, you will quickly find your peace of mind disturbed. They're only words, ideas, but you're so easily upset.

Our minds are incredible. Our ups and downs have nothing to

do with reality, nothing to do with the truth. It's very important to understand the psychology of this.

It's common for us to think that our own path and ideas are good, worthwhile and perfect, but by focusing excessively on this, we subconsciously put other paths and ideas down.

Perhaps I think, "Yellow is a fantastic color," and explain to you in great detail how yellow is good. Then, because of all my logical reasons, you too start think, "Yellow is good; yellow is the perfect color." But this automatically causes contradictory beliefs, "Blue is not so good; red is not so good," to arise in your mind.

There are two things in conflict with one another. This is common, but it's a mistake, especially when it comes to religion. We should not allow such contradictions in our mind where, by accepting one thing, we automatically reject another. If you check, you'll see it's not that you're blindly following something external but that your mind is too extreme in one direction. This automatically sets up the other extreme in opposition, and conflict between the two unbalances your mind and disturbs your inner peace.

This is how religious partisanship arises. You say, "I belong to this religion," and when you meet someone belonging to another, you feel insecure. This means your knowledge-wisdom is weak. You don't understand your mind's true nature and cling to an extreme point of view. Don't allow your mind to be polluted in this way; make sure you're mentally healthy. After all, the purpose of the practice of religion, Buddhism, Dharma, meditation or whatever else you want to call it is for you to take your mind completely beyond unhealthy, contradictory mental attitudes.

Lord Buddha himself exhorted the students he was teaching to practice without attachment. Although he taught a precise, incredible universal method, he made his students promise not to be attached to his teachings or to realizations, inner freedom, nirvana or enlightenment itself.

To achieve freedom from attachment is a very difficult thing, especially in a materialistic society. It's almost impossible for you to deal with material things without attachment and this causes you to bring a grasping attitude to spiritual matters. But even though it's difficult, you need to check how Lord Buddha's psychology offers you perfect mental health, free of extremes of this or that.

In our ordinary, samsaric, worldly life, we so easily get attached to and grasp at things we like, and nobody ever tells us to avoid attachment. But Lord Buddha, even though he offered his students the highest method to reach the highest goal, always admonished his students never to be attached to any of it. He said, "If you have the slightest attachment to me or my teachings, you're not only psychologically ill but you'll also destroy any chance you have of attaining complete and perfect enlightenment."

Also, he never told people to be biased towards his path or that following his path was good and following others was bad. In fact, one of the bodhisattva vows he made his followers take is the promise not to criticize the teachings of any other religion. Check why he did this; it shows how perfectly he understood human psychology. If it had been us, we'd have been saying, "I'm teaching you the highest, most perfect method. All the others are nothing." We treat the spiritual path in exactly the same competitive way that we do material pursuits, and if we keep acting this way, we'll never be mentally healthy or discover nirvana or everlasting, peaceful enlightenment. What, then, is the point of our spiritual practice?

Check up. Even in your samsaric, worldly life activities and relationships, the moment you get one idea or choose one thing, "This is so good," a contradiction automatically comes into your mind. When you're in love in the worldly, selfish way, check to see if your mind is too extreme or not; you'll find that it is.

Similarly, you should also avoid extremes when practicing your spiritual path. Of course, that shouldn't stop you practicing Dharma, or meditation; you still have to act. Just practice according to your own level of understanding.

That also doesn't mean that your mind should be closed to other religions. You can study any religion; you can check it out. The problem is that when you choose one particular religion, you get too extreme about its ideas and then put other religions and philosophies down. This happens because you don't know the purpose of religion, why it exists or how to practice. If you did, you'd never feel insecure about other religions. Not knowing the nature of other religions or their purpose makes you fear practitioners of other paths. If you understand that different people's minds need different methods and solutions, you'll see why there's a need for many religions.

It's really worthwhile for you to understand this basic psychology. Then, even in your everyday life, when people say you're good or bad, you won't go up and down; you'll know that it's not what people say that makes you good or bad. If, however, you find yourself going up and down according to what people say, you should recognize that this is happening because your mind is polluted; you're not seeing reality. Because of this, your relative, mundane judgments are labeling things good and bad and your mind is going up and down accordingly. Your up and down comes from your mind's making you believe those things really are good or bad. That's why you go up and down.

If you refuse to believe that superficial view, there'll no longer be any reason for you to go up and down when somebody says "good" or "bad." Words are not reality; ideas are not reality. Forget about your mind's ultimate nature; if you understand even its relative nature, there's no way anybody can make you go up and down by what they say. Even with this more superficial level of understanding, you discover a degree of truth within yourself.

A great deal of our suffering arises because we are conflicted about reputation. Instead of being concerned about the reality of what we are, we're concerned about what other people think of us. We're too outward looking. That's incredible. As far as Buddhism is concerned, that's a sick mind; totally, clinically sick.

Of course, Western psychologists don't consider that to be mental illness. Their terminology is different. Why is there this difference? It's because Lord Buddha's approach teaches us to seek the highest goal—everlasting, internal, indestructible peace of mind—and only when we attain that level of mind does Buddhism no longer consider us sick. Before that, our mind is liable to ups and downs and is therefore still sick, and we need more medicine: meditation, Dharma practice or whatever you want to call it. This is truly deep, profound psychology.

Western psychologists are satisfied that you're not clinically sick if you're well enough to conduct your everyday affairs, communicate with your friends and so forth. They're like, "OK, you can go now"! They're easily satisfied. But the supreme psychologist, Lord Buddha, looks deeper. He sees what's going on in the deep unconscious. Western psychologists are proud of where they've reached but say that, despite having made many advances, with respect to understanding the nature of the unconscious mind, they still have a long way to go. I read this in a psychology book.

Anyway, the reality is that you get attached to any idea that you think to be good, so even though the teachings of your spiritual path might in fact be good, try to practice them without attachment.

Sometimes you see people whose beliefs are too extreme, out on the street distributing religious literature. Even if you're busy, rushing somewhere, they stop you: "Here, read this." They so badly want to spread their ideas that they even preach in shopping centers and malls. This is too extreme. It's not necessary to do that. The mind needs time to absorb any idea. If you really want to teach somebody something, you have to wait until the person's ready and then do it. If somebody's mind is not ready, you shouldn't try to push your religious ideas onto that person, no matter how strongly you believe in them. It's like giving a dying person a precious jewel.

Many religions teach the importance of universal love, but the question is, how to develop that within yourself. You can't actualize universal love simply by reciting "universal love, universal love, universal love." Therefore, how do you gain that realization?

According to Lord Buddha, the first step is to develop a balanced mind towards all living beings; before you can attain universal love, you have to feel equilibrium with all beings in the universe. Therefore, the first thing to do is to train in equilibrium, and you're just dreaming if you think you can develop universal love without it.

Otherwise, you think that universal love is a wonderful idea, but at the same time are fanatical about the religion you've adopted. You have the fixed idea, "This is my religion." When somebody from another faith comes along, you feel uncomfortable; there's conflict in your mind. Then where's your universal love? Although you think it's fantastic, you can't manifest it because your mind is unbalanced. For universal love to come into your mind, you have to develop the feeling of equilibrium with all beings in the universe.

But that's easier said than done, so perhaps I should explain how to develop equilibrium. We do it in sitting meditation. Visualize in front of you a person who makes you agitated; someone you don't like. Visualize behind you the person to whom you are most attached. And visualize all around you the people to whom you feel indifferent; those who are not friends, relatives or enemies. Look at these three classes of person—friend, enemy and stranger—and meditate; see how you feel about each. When you look at your dear friend, a clinging feeling comes up; you want to go in that direction. When you look at the person who hurts and bothers you, you want to turn away; you reject that person.

This is a very simple way of checking how you feel about different people; it's not complicated. Just visualize them and see how you feel. Then ask yourself, "Why do I feel differently about different people? Why do I want to help the person I like and not the one I hate?" If you're honest, you'll find that your answers are the completely unreasonable responses of a deluded mind.

What this means is that you don't really understand the impermanent nature of human relationships. Those who know the real, true nature of the human mind understand that relationships are completely changeable and that there's no such thing as a permanent relationship; it's impossible. Even though you want it. But check back through the entire history of life on Earth, from the time it began up to now: where is that permanent relationship? When has there ever been a permanent relationship? It should still be here. But it's not, because there's no such thing.

Moreover, your judgment of people as friend, enemy and stranger is a complete misconception. For one thing, it's based on totally illogical reasons. Whatever your reasons, your feelings of "I like him, I don't like her" are totally illogical. They have nothing whatsoever to do with the true nature of either subject or object.

By judging people the way you do, you're like a person who has two extremely thirsty people coming to the door begging for water, and then arbitrarily choosing one, "You, please come in," and rejecting the other: "You, go away." That's exactly what you're like. If you really check up with introspective knowledge-wisdom, you'll see that your judgment of good and bad comes from concern for only your own selfish pleasure and never the pleasure of others.

Check up: visualize all universal living beings around you and realize that equally, just like you, they all want happiness and don't want unhappiness. Therefore, there's no reason to make the psychological distinction between friend and enemy, wanting to help the friend with extreme attachment, and wanting to give up on the bothersome, conflict—generating enemy with extreme dislike. That kind of mind is completely unrealistic, because as the dissatisfied human mind goes up and down, those kinds of relationship naturally change.

Even if you do want to feel angry toward another, it's the person's deluded mind you should be upset with, not his physical body. His mind is uncontrolled; he has no choice. When he attacks you, he's being driven by uncontrolled attachment or anger; that's what you should be angry at.

If somebody hits you with a car, you don't get angry at the car, do you? You get upset with the driver. It's exactly the same thing. The inner driver is the person's dissatisfied mind, not the symptoms of his emotions. Therefore, it's not your enemy himself but his delusions that you should be angry at. What a person says or does is simply symptomatic of what's in his mind.

Anyway, that's the approach to developing equilibrium, and the more you practice it, the more you'll realize that in reality, there's no reason to distinguish sentient beings as friend, enemy and stranger on the basis of the extremes of attachment and hatred; only an unhealthy mind does so. And when you do experience equilibrium, you'll be amazed at how your view of your enemy changes. The person who agitated and bothered you appears completely different—not because he has changed but because your mind has; you've changed your perception. This is not a fairy tale; this is reality.

When you change your attitude, your view of the sense world changes as well. When your mind is foggy, the world about you seems foggy; when your mind is clear, the world about you appears beautiful. You know this from your own experience. Your view of the world comes from your mind; it's a reflection of your mind. There's no permanent, perfectly good thing in the world. Where could you find such a thing? It's impossible.

You have to know your own psychology, how your mind works, how you discriminate between sentient beings because of unrealistic, illogical reasons. Therefore, you need to meditate. To discover universal love within your mind, you have to develop a feeling of equilibrium with all living beings in the universe. Once you've developed equilibrium, you don't have to worry about universal love; it will come automatically. That's how human psychology works. It's not something you can force: "Oh, universal love. I become you; you become me." What is that? Don't think that way.

When your mind is balanced with an equal feeling for all living beings, you'll automatically be happy. You won't have to say,

"I need happiness." You'll automatically be peaceful and happy, and furthermore, your body and speech will generate a peaceful vibration that will automatically benefit others, beyond words. Wherever you go, that vibration will be with you. But it's impossible to reach that level without meditation. Without meditating, you can't release any attachments, either spiritual or material, let alone experience universal love.

The Mahayana way of bringing the mind to enlightenment is gradual. As we have seen, in order to develop universal love, we first have to develop equilibrium. On this basis, we generate the bodhisattva's mind of enlightenment, bodhicitta, and having done so, our duty is to actualize the six perfections of charity, morality, patience, effort, concentration, and wisdom.

All religions emphasize the importance of charity, but Lord Buddha's approach differs from most in that he explains mainly the psychological aspect of giving and is not so interested in the externals of it. Why? Because the perfection of giving is realized only when we completely release the mind of miserly attachment, and this is a purely mental thing.

Many people think, with arrogance and pride, that they're religious because they give a lot of material things away, but this is very superficial. Such people have no idea of the essence of charity; just a vague notion that charity is good. They don't really know what it is. To engage in the bodhisattva's practice of charity is extremely difficult; it has to be done without a trace of miserliness.

Many people give with pride and attachment. That's not charity; it's just ego and, basically, not virtue. The bodhisattva's practice of charity—or, in fact, any of the six perfections—has to include the other five. In other words, charity must be practiced together with morality, patience, energy, concentration and wisdom—especially the latter. We need to have a profound understanding of emptiness in what we call the circle of the three: the emptiness of the object we're giving, the action of giving and the recipient of our gift. If we give without such understanding, it is neither beneficial nor perfect and, furthermore, can bring a conflicted reaction.

For example, if we're not free of attachment, we might give something to somebody today, and tomorrow be thinking, "I wish I hadn't given him that; now I need it." This kind of giving has nothing whatsoever to do with religion.

We might see people making charity and think how wonderfully generous they are, but all we see is the external action. We don't see their inner motivation, which can be totally berserk and selfish. The actual definition of religious giving is made according to the donor's mental attitude, not his or her physical actions.

If your giving weakens your disturbing negative attitudes and brings more peace and understanding into your mind, it's religious, but if it serves merely to increase your delusions, you're better off not doing it, no matter how it appears from the outside. Why do something that exacerbates your already agitated mind? Be realistic; know what you're doing.

If you do your spiritual practice with understanding, it will be really worthwhile and effective and bring the results you seek.

Even simply feeling equilibrium with all living beings—not discriminating others as friend, enemy, and stranger—can bring you great happiness and freedom from insecurity.

We often feel bothered by others, but we have to realize that seeing them as enemies comes from us, not them. There's no such thing as a born enemy. We make it all up. There's no such thing as permanent evil. Actual evil is the negative mind that projects evil outside; a positive mind will label the same thing good. Things always change; permanent evil is totally non-existent.

Also, when we're depressed, we think, "I'm bad, I'm negative, I'm sinful," but that's complete nonsense; an exaggerated extreme. We have both positive and negative within us; it's simply a question of which is stronger at any given time. That's what we have to check. Therefore, whenever our mind gives us trouble, it's a sign that we're thinking in extremes.

This is where meditation comes in. Meditation means investigating the mind to see what's going on. When we do it properly, we purify and bring peace into our unbalanced mind. That's the function of meditation; that's the function of religion. Therefore, we should meditate as correctly as possible.

One thing to avoid on the spiritual path is jumping at ideas. Instead, try to find the key to putting ideas into your experience. Experiencing their meaning is much more important than the ideas themselves. For example, we should not make charity of things that belong to other people, like our family and friends. I've often heard of young people taking things from their parents, like their mother's jewels, and giving them away to beggars in the street.

That's strange; it's not charity. And I've often been asked if it's OK to steal from the rich to give to the poor. That's not charity either.

The ordinary understanding of charity is giving things to others, but as you can see, the Buddhist point of view is that material giving is not necessarily charity. True charity has to do with the mind; giving mentally. The practice of giving is training the mind to overcome miserliness. Miserly attachment is in the mind, therefore, the antidote must also be mental.

Another thing is that, when it comes to giving, sometimes we're extreme. We don't check to see if the recipient needs what we're giving; we just give without hesitation. However, sometimes it may not be beneficial; in such cases, it's better not to give. If what you give creates problems and, instead of being helped, the recipient experiences harm, it's not charity. You think your action is positive, but it's negative.

If you really, deeply check up what true charity is, you'll probably find that in your whole life you've never performed even one act of charity. Have you really checked the recipient's needs? Have you generated the right motivation before giving? Have you performed the action with meditation on the circle of the three? And if you've given with pride, then no matter how great your gift, it's been wasted; your giving's been a joke.

Thus, you can see how difficult perfect charity can be. I'm not just being negative; I'm being realistic. Make sure that whatever you do becomes worthwhile. If you practice with understanding, it can be powerful and psychologically effective, have real meaning and, without doubt, bring the peaceful realizations you desire. On the other hand, if you do your practices half-heartedly and without understanding, all you'll get is depressed.

Therefore, don't think that charity is physical—it's mental. Charity is turning the mind away from and releasing miserly attachment. That's fantastic. It's meditation, a psychological state of mind and very effective.

You should also avoid making charity of things that hurt others. For example, you shouldn't donate to war efforts. Sometimes you might be asked to give money to people fighting in the name of religion, but how can supporting war be spiritual? It's impossible. You have to check carefully that your charitable giving does not bring harm.

It's extremely difficult to practice Dharma such that it diminishes your delusions, but if you can, it's most worthwhile; it will really shake your ego. Even one small act of charitable giving motivated by the intention to realize everlasting, peaceful enlightenment can be incredibly effective and really shatter your attachment.

There are three kinds of charity: giving material objects, giving knowledge-wisdom, and saving others from danger. You should do whichever of these you can, with as much understanding as possible, according to your ability.

The ultimate aim of charity is perfect enlightenment, so you should dedicate your acts of charity to this goal. But we don't do that, do we? If somebody's cold, we just toss him a blanket— "Warm enough? OK, good"—and leave it at that. If someone's thirsty, we just give her a drink—"Thirst finished? OK, good"— and that that's the end of it. Our goals are so temporal and shortsighted that our giving becomes just another material trip. Our understanding of charity is too superficial. Instead, we should help others with temporal needs by understanding that in order to reach enlightenment, they need a healthy body and mind, and give in order to help their Dharma practice, dedicating our merit to the enlightenment of all sentient beings.

I'm not just being negative; I'm talking about the way we are. And I'm sure that if you practice properly, you can definitely attain everlasting, peaceful enlightenment. But even forgetting about that, if you practice well today, tomorrow you'll automatically be more peaceful; if you meditate properly in the morning, your whole day goes more smoothly. You can easily experience the truth of this. However, attaining enlightenment through meditating, practicing the six perfections and advancing through the ten bodhisattva stages is a gradual process.

When we do become enlightened, we'll no longer have feelings of partiality. If Lord Buddha had one person angrily stabbing his right arm with a knife and another devotedly anointing his left with scented oil, he wouldn't have hatred for the one and craving desire for the other. He would feel equal love for both—the love an enlightened being feels for others is universal and completely impartial.

Our love, however, is completely selfish. We get attached to people who are nice to us and dislike those who treat us badly. Our minds are extremely unbalanced.

My conclusion is that we should not be attached to anything, not even our religion, much less material things. We should practice our spiritual path understanding its reality and how it relates to us as individuals. That's the way to discover universal love, free of insecure, partisan feelings such as, "I'm a Buddhist," "I'm a Christian," "I'm a Hindu," or whatever. It doesn't matter what we are; each of us has to find the path that suits us as individuals.

Some people like rice; others like potatoes; others something else. Let people eat whatever they like, whatever satisfies their body. You can't say, "I don't like rice; nobody should eat rice." It's the same thing with religion.

If you have this kind of understanding, you'll never be against any religion. Different people need different paths. Let them do what they need to do. But unfortunately, our limited minds aren't that relaxed. We think, "My religion is the best, the only way. All the others are wrong." Holding such fixed preconceptions means we are sick. It's not religions that are at fault; it's their followers. Therefore, if you want to be psychologically healthy, understand your path and act correctly and realizations will come of their own accord.

Now, before I finish, I want to make one thing clear. I'm not criticizing anybody; I'm not putting anybody's practice down. But these days, most of us grow up in societies that don't offer many opportunities for the serious study and practice of religion. Therefore, it's important that when you practice Dharma, you do so properly and don't turn your practice into just another worldly pursuit. The modern world thinks material development is extremely important and gives short shrift to the development of a peaceful mind. Of course, if somebody actually asks you, "Do you think spiritual pursuits are important?" you're going to say, "Yes, but…." There's always a "but, but, but" involved. That shows how we really are.

Q. If we don't have many monks at the time and place where we are born, is that the result of bad karma?
Lama. I don't think so. That's like saying that it's bad karma not to be a monk. It's not like that. You don't have to be a monk or nun to be knowledgeable. You can't say that people in robes are higher than those who are not. You can't judge things in that way. It's entirely up to the individual. Perhaps you can say, however, that it's individual bad karma to find yourself in a situation where you can't understand your own mind and mental attitudes or discover true, inner peace and satisfaction.

Q. Lama, when we're doing meditation, how do we know that the thinker and the thought are the same? That the thinker is the thought; that the thinker is not separate from the thought?
Lama. Relatively, the thinker is not the thought. The thinker is just "name" and, at that time, thought is just "functioning." But if you can completely integrate yourself with thought when you're meditating, that's a good experience. However, from the standpoint of relative truth and scientific understanding, person and thought are different. You are not thought. Even if in meditation you feel complete oneness with your thought, still, you and thought are not the same thing. Although at the absolute level there's unity, relatively, there's a difference. But when you medi-

tate, if you feel complete oneness with all universal phenomena, if you feel that your physical being is like a single atom but your nature is totally unified with the energy of the whole universe, that's a good experience.

Also, when you're trying to concentrate on one thing and other thoughts keep coming, instead of rejecting them, trying to push them away, think, "You're welcome," and investigate them with penetrating, introspective knowledge-wisdom, looking into the nature of your thoughts' reality. Thoughts are silly; when you look at them, they disappear. They're just kidding; when you analyze them, they vanish. Up until now, the more you've tried to push them away, the more they've kept on coming at you. Try welcoming them.

Actually, watching your thoughts is much more interesting than watching TV. TV's boring; it's the same old thing over and over again. When you observe your mind, incredibly different things appear. You have an amazing collection of memories; after all these years, even childhood memories surface. TV's never that interesting.

When you understand the way your mind works, that's the beginning of control. You'll stop getting upset when thoughts appear; psychologically, you'll know what they mean. Somebody who has no idea of what the mind is or how it works gets shocked when the unconscious mind suddenly manifests at the conscious level: "Oh! What's that?" When you understand your mind and what's in it, you expect that sort of thing to happen. You understand the nature of your mind and have a solution for its dark side. If you think that you're completely pure and then suddenly some ugly mind arises, you freak out. However, you also have to understand that you're not completely negative. Your mind has both a positive and a negative nature. But it's all relative, coming and going like clouds in the sky. But underneath it all, your real, true nature remains completely pure, unchanged like the sky itself. Therefore, to be human is to be powerful; we have the ability to do great things because our fundamental nature is positive.

Thank you very much, thank you.

Chinese Buddhist Society, Sydney, 24 April 1975

GLOSSARY

(Skt = Sanskrit; Tib = Tibetan)

Atisha (924-1054). The great Indian master renowned for his practice of bodhicitta who came to Tibet to help revive Buddhism and spent the last seventeen years of his life there. His seminal text, *A Lamp for the Path to Enlightenment,* initiated the steps of the path (*Tib: lam-rim*) tradition found in all schools of Tibetan Buddhism. Founder of the Kadampa school, fore-runner of the Gelug.

bodhicitta (Skt). The altruistic determination to reach enlightenment for the sole purpose of enlightening all sentient beings.

bodhisattva (Skt). Someone whose spiritual practice is directed towards the achievement of enlightenment for the sake of all sentient beings. One who, with the compassionate motivation of bodhicitta, follows the Mahayana path through ten levels to enlightenment.

buddha (Skt). A fully enlightened being. One who has removed all obscurations veiling the mind and has developed all good qualities to perfection. The first of the Three Jewels of Refuge. See also *enlightenment, Shakyamuni Buddha.*

cyclic existence (Skt: samsara; Tib: khor-wa). The six realms of conditioned existence, three lower—hell, hungry ghost (*Skt: preta*) and animal—and three upper—human, demigod (*Skt: asura*) and god (*Skt: sura*). It is the beginningless, recurring cycle of death and rebirth under the control of delusion and karma and fraught with suffering. It also refers to the contaminated aggregates of a sentient being.

Dharma (Skt). Spiritual teachings, particularly those of Shakyamuni Buddha. Literally, that which holds one back from suffering. The second of the Three Jewels of Refuge.

dualistic view. The ignorant view characteristic of the unenlightened mind in which all things are falsely conceived to have concrete self-existence. To such a view, the appearance of an object is mixed with the false image of its being independent or self-existent, thereby leading to further dualistic views concerning subject and object, self and other, this and that and so forth.

ego-mind. The wrong conception, "I am self-existent." Ignorance of the nature of the mind and self.

eight worldly dharmas. The eight mundane concerns for gain, loss, fame, notoriety, praise, blame, happiness and suffering.

enlightenment (Skt: bodhi). Full awakening; buddhahood. The ultimate goal of Buddhist practice, attained when all limitations have been removed from the mind and one's positive potential has been completely and perfectly realized. It is a state characterized by infinite compassion, wisdom and skill.

four noble truths. The truths of suffering, the origin of suffering, the cessation of suffering and the path to the cessation of suffering; the topic of the first turning of the wheel of Dharma— the first discourse ever given by the Buddha.

Gelug/Kagyu/Sakya/Nyingma. The four main schools of Tibetan Buddhism. Lama Yeshe belonged to the Gelug school.

geshe. A monk who has completed a full monastic education in Buddhist philosophy and debate, passed an examination at the end and been awarded a *geshe* degree.

hallucinate. Lama Yeshe's use does not refer to chemically- or illness-induced hallucinations but to inappropriate projections by the ignorant mind. See *superstition*.

Hinayana (Skt). Literally, Small, or Lesser, Vehicle. It is one of the two general divisions of Buddhism. Hinayana practitioners' motivation for following the Dharma path is principally their intense wish for personal liberation from conditioned existence, or samsara. Two types of Hinayana practitioner are identified: hearers and solitary realizers. Cf. *Mahayana*.

Kadampa. School of Tibetan Buddhism founded in the eleventh century by Atisha and his followers, principally his interpreter, Drom-tön-ba.

kalpa (*Skt*). Eon. According to Shakyamuni Buddha, longer than the amount of time it would take a cube of solid granite to be worn away by being stroked lightly with a piece of fine silk once every hundred years.

lam-rim (*Tib*). The graduated path. A presentation of Shakyamuni Buddha's teachings in a form suitable for the step-by-step training of a disciple. The lam-rim was first formulated by the great India teacher Atisha (Dipamkara Shrijnana, 982-1055) when he came to Tibet in 1042. See also *three principal paths*.

Mahayana (*Skt*). Literally, Great Vehicle. It is one of the two general divisions of Buddhism. Mahayana practitioners' motivation for following the Dharma path is principally their intense wish that all sentient beings be liberated from conditioned existence, or samsara, and attain the full enlightenment of buddhahood. The Mahayana has two divisions, Paramitayana (Sutrayana) and Vajrayana (Tantrayana, Mantrayana). Cf. *Hinayana*.

mind (*Skt: citta; Tib: sem*). Synonymous with consciousness (*Skt: vijnana; Tib: nam-she*) and sentience (*Skt: manas; Tib: yi*). Defined as that which is "clear and knowing"; a formless entity that has the ability to perceive objects. Mind is divided into six primary consciousnesses and fifty-one mental factors.

Nagarjuna (*Skt*). The second century A.D. Indian Buddhist philosopher who propounded the Madhyamaka philosophy of emptiness.

Padmasambhava (*Tib: Guru Rinpoche*). Indian tantric master invited to Tibet by King Trisong Detsen in the eighth century. Founder of the Nyingma school of Tibetan Buddhism.

refuge. The door to the Dharma path. A Buddhist takes refuge in the Three Jewels fearing the sufferings of samsara and having faith that Buddha, Dharma and Sangha have the power to lead him or her out of suffering to happiness, liberation or enlightenment.

Sangha (*Skt*). Spiritual community; the third of the Three Jewels of Refuge. Absolute Sangha are those who have directly realized emptiness; relative Sangha are ordained monks and nuns.

Shakyamuni Buddha (563-483 BC). Fourth of the one thousand founding buddhas of this present world age. Born Siddhartha Gotama, a prince of the Shakya clan in north India, he taught the sutra and tantra paths to liberation and enlightenment; founder of what came to be known as Buddhism. (From the *Skt: buddha*— "fully awake.")

shunyata (*Skt*). Emptiness. The absence of all false ideas about how things exist; specifically, the lack of the apparent independent, self-existence of phenomena.

six perfections (*Skt: paramita*). Charity, morality, patience, enthusiastic perseverance, concentration and wisdom.

superstition (*Tib: nam-tog*). Erroneous belief about reality.

three lower realms. The three realms of greatest suffering in cyclic existence, comprising the animal, hungry ghost (*Skt: preta*) and hell realms.

three principal paths. The three main divisions of the lam-rim: renunciation, bodhicitta and right view.

Tsong Khapa, Lama Je (1357-1417). Founder of the Gelug tradition of Tibetan Buddhism and revitalizer of many sutra and tantra lineages and the monastic tradition in Tibet.

yana (*Skt*). Literally, vehicle. An inner vehicle that carries you along the spiritual path to enlightenment. Buddhism is divided into two main vehicles, *Hinayana* and *Mahayana*.

LAMA YESHE WISDOM ARCHIVE

The LAMA YESHE WISDOM ARCHIVE (LYWA) is the collected works of Lama Thubten Yeshe and Lama Thubten Zopa Rinpoche. The ARCHIVE was founded in 1996 by Lama Zopa Rinpoche, its spiritual director, to make available in various ways the teachings it contains. Distribution of free booklets of edited teachings is one of the ways.

Lama Yeshe and Lama Zopa Rinpoche began teaching at Kopan Monastery, Nepal, in 1970. Since then, their teachings have been recorded and transcribed. At present the LYWA contains more than 7,000 cassette tapes, all of which have now been digitized, and approximately 50,000 pages of transcribed teachings on computer disk. Many tapes, mostly teachings by Lama Zopa Rinpoche, remain to be transcribed. As Rinpoche continues to teach, the number of tapes in the ARCHIVE increases accordingly. Most of the transcripts have been neither checked nor edited.

Here at LYWA we are making every effort to organize the transcription of that which has not yet been transcribed, to edit that which has not yet been edited, and generally to do the many other tasks detailed as follows. In all this, we need your help. Please contact us for more information:

LAMA YESHE WISDOM ARCHIVE
PO Box 356, Weston, MA 02493, USA
Telephone (781) 259-4466; Fax (413) 845-9239
info@LamaYeshe.com
www.LamaYeshe.com

THE ARCHIVE TRUST

The work of the LAMA YESHE WISDOM ARCHIVE falls into two categories: archiving and dissemination.

ARCHIVING requires managing the audiotapes of teachings by Lama Yeshe and Lama Zopa Rinpoche that have already been collected, collecting recordings of teachings given but not yet sent to the ARCHIVE, and collecting recordings of Lama Zopa's on-going teachings, talks, advice and so forth as he travels the world for the benefit of all. Tapes and disks are then catalogued and stored safely while being kept accessible for further work.

We organize the transcription of tapes, add the transcripts to the already existent database of teachings, manage this database, have transcripts checked, and make transcripts available to editors or others doing research on or practicing these teachings.

Other archiving activities include working with videotapes and photographs of the Lamas and digitizing ARCHIVE materials.

DISSEMINATION involves making the Lamas' teachings available directly or indirectly through various avenues such as booklets for free distribution, regular books for the trade, lightly edited transcripts, floppy disks, audio- and videotapes and CDs, and articles in Mandala and other magazines, and on our Web site. Irrespective of the method we choose, the teachings require a significant amount of work to prepare them for distribution.

This is just a summary of what we do. The ARCHIVE was established with virtually no seed funding and has developed solely through the kindness of many people, some of whom we have mentioned at the front of this book and most of the others on our Web site. We sincerely thank them all.

Our further development similarly depends upon the generosity of those who see the benefit and necessity of this work, and we would be extremely grateful for your help.

THE ARCHIVE TRUST has been established to fund the above activities and we hereby appeal to you for your kind support. If you would like to make a contribution to help us with any of the above tasks or to sponsor booklets for free distribution, please contact us at our Weston address.

The LAMA YESHE WISDOM ARCHIVE is a 501(c)(3) tax-deductible, non-profit corporation (ID number 04-3374479) dedicated to the welfare of all sentient beings and totally dependent upon your donations for its continued existence.

Thank you so much for your support. You may contribute by mailing a check, bank draft or money order to our Weston address; by making a donation on our secure Web site; by mailing or faxing us your credit card number or by phoning it in; or by transferring funds directly to our bank—ask us for details.

THE FOUNDATION FOR THE PRESERVATION OF THE MAHAYANA TRADITION

The Foundation for the Preservation of the Mahayana Tradition (FPMT) is an international organization of Buddhist meditation study and retreat centers, both urban and rural, monasteries, publishing houses, healing centers and other related activities founded in 1975 by Lama Thubten Yeshe and Lama Thubten Zopa Rinpoche. At present, there are more than 150 FPMT activities in over thirty countries worldwide.

The FPMT has been established to facilitate the study and practice of Mahayana Buddhism in general and the Tibetan Gelug tradition, founded in the fifteenth century by the great scholar, yogi and saint, Lama Je Tsong Khapa, in particular.

Every three months, the Foundation publishes a magazine, *Mandala*, from its International Office in the United States of America. To subscribe or view back issues, please go to the *Mandala* Web site, www.mandalamagazine.org, or contact:

FPMT
PO Box 888, Taos, NM 87571, USA
Telephone (505) 758-7766; fax (505) 758-7765
fpmtinfo@fpmt.org
www.fpmt.org

Our Web site also offers teachings by His Holiness the Dalai Lama, Lama Yeshe, Lama Zopa Rinpoche and many other highly respected teachers in the tradition, details about the FPMT's educational programs, audio through FPMT radio, a complete listing of FPMT centers all over the world and in your area, and links to FPMT centers on the Web, where you will find details of their programs, and to other interesting Buddhist and Tibetan home pages.

Lama Zopa Rinpoche
Teachings from the Vajrasattva Retreat
Edited by Ailsa Cameron and Nicholas Ribush

This book is an edited transcript of Rinpoche's teachings during the Vajrasattva retreat at Land of Medicine Buddha, California, February through April, 1999. It contains explanations of the various practices done during the retreat, such as Vajrasattva purification, prostrations to the Thirty-five Buddhas, Lama Chöpa, making light offerings, liberating animals and much, much more. There are also many weekend public lectures covering general topics such as compassion and emptiness. The appendices detail several of the practices taught, for example, the short Vajrasattva sadhana, light offerings, liberating animals and making charity of water to Dzambhala and the pretas.

It is essential reading for all Lama Zopa Rinpoche's students, especially retreat leaders and FPMT center spiritual program coordinators, and serious Dharma students everywhere.

704 pp., detailed table of contents, 7 appendices
6" x 9" paperback
ISBN 1-891868-04-7
US$20 & shipping and handling

Available from the LYWA, Wisdom Publications (Boston), Wisdom Books (London), Mandala Books (Melbourne), Snow Lion Publications (USA) and FPMT centers everywhere. Discount for bookstores. Free for members of the International Mahayana Institute.

OTHER TEACHINGS OF
LAMA YESHE AND LAMA ZOPA RINPOCHE
CURRENTLY AVAILABLE

BOOKS PUBLISHED BY WISDOM PUBLICATIONS

Wisdom Energy, by Lama Yeshe and Lama Zopa Rinpoche
Introduction to Tantra, by Lama Yeshe
Transforming Problems, by Lama Zopa Rinpoche
The Door to Satisfaction, by Lama Zopa Rinpoche
The Tantric Path of Purification, by Lama Yeshe
The Bliss of Inner Fire, by Lama Yeshe
Becoming the Compassion Buddha, by Lama Yeshe

You may see more information about and order the above titles at the Wisdom Web site, www.wisdompubs.org, or call toll free in the USA on 1-800-272-4050.

TRANSCRIPTS

Several transcripts of teachings by Lama Yeshe and Lama Zopa Rinpoche are also available. See the LAMA YESHE WISDOM ARCHIVE Web site for more details.

VIDEOS OF LAMA YESHE

We are in the process of converting our VHS videos of Lama Yeshe's teachings to DVD. *The Three Principal Aspects of the Path* and *Introduction to Tantra* are currently available. See our Web site for more information.

VIDEOS OF LAMA ZOPA RINPOCHE

See the FPMT Web site for more information. You will also find there many recommended practices written or compiled by Rinpoche.

What to do with Dharma teachings

The Buddhadharma is the true source of happiness for all sentient beings. Books like the one in your hand show you how to put the teachings into practice and integrate them into your life, whereby you get the happiness you seek. Therefore, anything containing Dharma teachings or the names of your teachers is more precious than other material objects and should be treated with respect. To avoid creating the karma of not meeting the Dharma again in future lives, please do not put books (or other holy objects) on the floor or underneath other stuff, step over or sit upon them, or use them for mundane purposes such as propping up wobbly tables. They should be kept in a clean, high place, separate from worldly writings, and wrapped in cloth when being carried around. These are but a few considerations.

Should you need to get rid of Dharma materials, they should not be thrown in the rubbish but burned in a special way. Briefly: do not incinerate such materials with other trash, but alone, and as they burn, recite the mantra OM AH HUM. As the smoke rises, visualize that it pervades all of space, carrying the essence of the Dharma to all sentient beings in the six samsaric realms, purifying their minds, alleviating their suffering, and bringing them all happiness, up to and including enlightenment. Some people might find this practice a bit unusual, but it is given according to tradition. Thank you very much.

Dedication

Through the merit created by preparing, reading, thinking about and sharing this book with others, may all teachers of the Dharma live long and healthy lives, may the Dharma spread throughout the infinite reaches of space, and may all sentient beings quickly attain enlightenment.

In whichever realm, country, area or place this book may be, may there be no war, drought, famine, disease, injury, disharmony or unhappiness, may there be only great prosperity, may every thing needed be easily obtained, and may all be guided by only perfectly qualified Dharma teachers, enjoy the happiness of Dharma, have only love and compassion for all beings, and only benefit and never harm each other.

LAMA THUBTEN YESHE was born in Tibet in 1935. At the age of six, he entered the great Sera Monastic University, Lhasa, where he studied until 1959, when the Chinese invasion of Tibet forced him into exile in India. Lama Yeshe continued to study and meditate in India until 1967, when, with his chief disciple, Lama Thubten Zopa Rinpoche, he went to Nepal. Two years later he established Kopan Monastery, near Kathmandu, in order to teach Buddhism to Westerners. In 1974, the Lamas began making annual teaching tours to the West, and as a result of these travels a worldwide network of Buddhist teaching and meditation centers—the Foundation for the Preservation of the Mahayana Tradition—began to develop. In 1984, after an intense decade of imparting a wide variety of incredible teachings and establishing one FPMT activity after another, at the age of forty-nine, Lama Yeshe passed away. He was reborn as Osel Hita Torres in Spain in 1985, recognized as the incarnation of Lama Yeshe by His Holiness the Dalai Lama in 1986, and, as the monk Lama Tenzin Osel Rinpoche, is studying for his *geshe* degree at the reconstituted Sera Monastery in South India. Lama's remarkable story is told in Vicki Mackenzie's book, *Reincarnation: The Boy Lama* (Wisdom Publications, 1996). Some of Lama Yeshe's teachings have also been published by Wisdom and others are available on video. Details are a few pages back.

DR. NICHOLAS RIBUSH, MB, BS, is a graduate of Melbourne University Medical School (1964) who first encountered Buddhism at Kopan Monastery, Nepal, in 1972. Since then he has been a student of Lama Yeshe and Lama Zopa Rinpoche and a full time worker for their international organization, the Foundation for the Preservation of the Mahayana Tradition (FPMT). He was a monk from 1974 to 1986. He established FPMT archiving and publishing activities at Kopan in 1973, and with Lama Yeshe founded Wisdom Publications in 1975. Between 1981 and 1996 he served variously as Wisdom's director, editorial director and director of development. Over the years he has edited and published many teachings by Lama Yeshe and Lama Zopa Rinpoche, and established and/or directed several other FPMT activities, including the International Mahayana Institute, Tushita Mahayana Meditation Centre, the Enlightened Experience Celebration, Mahayana Publications, Kurukulla Center for Tibetan Buddhist Studies and now the LAMA YESHE WISDOM ARCHIVE. He was a member of the FPMT board of directors from its inception in 1983 until 2002.